MW00790574

Praise for the
The Joys of Dating

"*Why I Love Men* is a great book that really empowers women!"
—Jamie Foxx

"*Why I Love Men: The Joys of Dating* is filled with solid advice, helpful assessments and interesting stories that will change the way single women view dating and relationships. A must-read for women looking for love!"
—**Marci Shimoff, NY Times bestselling author of**
Happy for No Reason

"J.J. Smith cuts through the chatter with some tried-and-true cures to our relationship malaise. There are other books of this type but what separates J.J. Smith's book from the others is she dares to tell the raw truth about the power of sex. The book is written in a conversational tone that grabs the reader with charm, style, almost like an intimate whisper from a sista friend."
—**AALBC.com, the African American Literature**
Book Club

"Your dating book, *Why I Love Men: The Joys of Dating* is HOT!! Your book takes on the hottest topics and delivers relevant, modern answers for both the veteran homemaker and the savvy single. I really could not put the book down!"
—**Clayton A. Ivey, CFO, Express Business Services**

"If you enjoyed Steve Harvey's frank and funny Act Like a Lady, Think Like a Man, you will love this book! *Why I Love Men: The Joys of Dating* is extremely well written and provides excellent advice for single women of all colors. Read it!"
—**Bookideas.com**

"*Why I Love Men* is a wonderful guide for the single, heterosexual woman looking for tips on how to improve her chances on the dating scene. *Why I Love Men* provides an excellent resource for single women who believe they really need assistance and inspiration in their relationships with men."

—**BookReview.com rated** *Why I Love Men: The Joys of Dating* **as EXCELLENT!**

"I found *Why I Love Men* to offer a refreshing, up-to-date approach on dating. J.J. Smith also offers a wealth of advice on dating for women who are either getting back into the dating game or dissatisfied with their current dating situations. I HIGHLY recommend this book. I truly enjoyed reading *Why I Love Men* and found J.J. Smith's writing to be highly motivating and energizing."

—**ReaderViews.com**

"I just put down J.J. Smith's insightful new book *Why I Love Men: The Joys of Dating* and my first reaction is that J.J. Smith has got it going ON! She epitomizes style and class, and women everywhere, single or not, would do well to take her advice."

—**Bookideas.com**

"The information in *Why I Love Men: The Joys of Dating* is timely, relevant, informative, and funny. Your style of writing is intelligent, yet down-to-earth. Women between the ages of 18-45 will be able to relate."

—**Dwan**

"I don't really want women to know all of these things that J.J. tells them, as it gives away our (men's) secrets."

—**Todd**

"J.J. is so inspiring and motivating. I loved the fact that she shared so much of herself with us. I don't read much and I read the whole book in one weekend. The tips, suggestions, and assessments motivated me to really improve myself."

—**Mary**

why i
love men

The Joys of Dating

J.J. Smith

why i love men
The Joys of Dating
by J.J. Smith

Published by Adiva Publishing
12138 Central Ave, Ste. 391
Mitchellville, MD 20721
Fax: 240-525-8016

For more information, see www.jjsmithonline.com.

Book Cover Design by George Foster
Interior Design by Irene Archer
Editing by Robin Quinn, Quinn's Word for Word
Author's Photo by Roy Cox Photography

DISCLAIMER: The author does not guarantee that any products or recommendations will provide you with the same benefits that she has achieved. You should seek a doctor and do your own research to determine if any of the products or recommendations made in this book by the author would work for you. Additionally, the author is not paid for any books or products that she recommends in this book. Additionally, the stories and names in this book have been modified or changed to not reveal the identity of any real person. Any resemblance of persons depicted in the stories in this book is strictly coincidental.

While the author has made every effort to provide accurate product names and contact information, such as Internet addresses, at the time of publication, neither the publisher nor the author assumes responsibility for errors, or changes that occur after publication. Additionally, the author does not have any control over products or websites associated with those products listed in this book or the content of those websites.

The book is sold with the understanding that the publisher is not engaged in rendering any legal, accounting, financial or other professional advice. If financial, legal or expert assistance is required, the services of a competent professional should be sought. The author and publisher shall have neither liability nor responsibility to any person, company or entity with respect to any loss or damage caused directly or indirectly by the concepts, ideas, products, information or suggested tasks presented in this book. By reading this book you agree to be bound to the statements above.

Library of Congress Cataloging-in-Publication Data

Smith, J.J.

Why I Love Men: The Joys of Dating /J.J. Smith, First Edition

1.Relationships/Self-Help   2. Dating   3. Love

ISBN: 978-0-9823018-0-7

Library of Congress Control Number: 2009901785

Contents

Introduction . . . . *xi*

PART I. THE JOYS AND PAINS OF RELATIONSHIPS 1

1. I Never Knew Eros (Sexual) Love Like This 3

2. Why I'm a S&M (Success and Money) Diva 19

3. Reaching My Beauty Potential 37

4. Strippin' Ain't Easy 51

5. I'm His Wife, Not His Girlfriend 59

PART II. THE DATING ACTION PLAN: Become the
Woman Every Man Wants 67

6. Unpack Your Baggage – *Learn from your past
    mistakes and move on with your life* 69

7. Love Yourself First – *Learn to love yourself and focus
    on your own happiness.* 73

8. Determine Your Relationship Market Value
    (RMV) – *Assess the personal strengths that you bring
    to a relationship before you begin dating.* 79

9. Fix Your Fatal Flaws – *Work on eliminating the habits
    and traits that make you less attractive to men.* 87

10. **Have a Life of Your Own** – *Have a purposeful,
fun-filled life* 91

11. **Begin Your Beauty Transformation** – *Maximize
your physical appearance* 99

12. **Embrace Your Sexuality** – *Understand the power
and pleasure of sex.* 107

13. **Two Necessities – A Good Job and Good Credit**: *Maintain both a successful career and financial
stability* 115

14. **Expand Your Circle of Friends, Hang Out with
Guys and Learn from Divas** – *Develop male friendships if you want to best understand men* 123

15. **Decide Whether to Accept a Role in His Life** –
*Will you be happy with the type of relationship he is
offering?... you decide.* 127

PART III. THE DATING ACTION PLAN: **Find the Man
that Every Woman Wants.** **133**

16. **Steer Clear of Unavailable Men** – *Avoid low-
percentage relationship options* 137

17. **Determine His Value to You** – *Be clear about what
you want in a mate and determine his value to you* . . 143

18. **Increase the Quantity and Quality of the Men
You Meet** – *Learn the best methods for meeting men
and increasing your number of dates* 151

19. Know Where and How to Date Him – *Determine good and bad first date locations, and learn how communication helps to secure the second date.* 165

20. Check Him Out – *Get to know who he is before you become too serious* 175

21. Learn to Stroke His Ego – *Learn to befriend his ego; avoid ego-busters* 181

PART IV. THE TRUTHS AND LESSONS LEARNED FROM DATING **185**

22. The Truth about Men 187

- Men Cheat on Women They Love

- Men Really Don't Want to Be Changed

- Don't Underestimate the Relationship between a Man and His Mother

- Cooking Is Still Important to Modern Men

- Kissing Tells You a Lot about His Feelings for You

23. The Truth about Love and Relationships 193

- Romantic Love Is the Number One Illusion for Single Women

- Relationships Are Opportunities for Spiritual Growth

- The Majority of Your Romantic Relationships WILL Come to an End – Prepare for It

24. The Truth about "Open" Relationships...........199

- Redefining Marriage Relationships
- Types of Open (Marriage) Relationships
- Impact of Open Marriages
- Is Open Marriage Adultery?
- Are Open Relationships or an Open Marriage Right for You?

25. Conclusion. Dating Is a Competitive Sport – *Learn to Enjoy It!* 209

Introduction

All women desire love. We all want to love and be loved. We all desire fulfilling relationships in our life that meet our spiritual, emotional and physical needs. And we all deserve to have healthy, satisfying love relationships in our life.

But how much time and money have we invested in creating a life that attracts the love we want and desire? A few years ago, I calculated the investment made in my career and professional development since college, and I was surprised to find that the figure was over $60,000. I realized that this huge amount had been spent on training programs to improve my skills in such areas as presentation, executive management, facilitation, writing and technical abilities in order to advance my career. I also saw that this investment had really paid off; today I enjoy a career as Vice President and Partner in an IT Consulting Firm. So I asked myself, What if I also invested time and money into my personal life? What if I spent time and money on learning what it takes to attract the type of men that are ideal for me? Would I get the results that I desire? Well, this book shares all that I have learned throughout my journey toward fulfilling love relationships.

Why did I write this book? Basically, it's because I love men. I find men to be attractive and fascinating. Men have shaped my life, and they've helped me to grow, learn and develop as a woman. Over my entire life, I have been surrounded by men. I grew up in a household with three brothers, and my mom and dad. My closest friends throughout my life have been men. Even today, my best friend is a man who I love dearly. Even where I currently work, I am surrounded by men. I have been consulting with a new client for the past year, and all day I am surrounded by four of the funniest, wittiest and most attractive men that I have ever met. Every day I think that I must be the luckiest woman in the world. They certainly make things at work enjoyable and fun.

I am grateful for the men who I have dated and loved over the years, those who have brought me joy and, yes, even those who have brought me pain. I am better today because of the presence of all of these men in my life.

Dating Is Very Competitive Today

Today's dating environment is extremely competitive. The odds are much better for men because they are outnumbered by women in every state, except for Alaska and Nevada. Nationally, there are 143.5 million females to 138 million males. For Black women, it is even more challenging. In our nation, there are 10 single Black women for every seven single Black men, and over 70% of Black women are single. So women have to be very deliberate about finding, attracting and keeping a good man.

Due to the challenges encountered when meeting and dating men, many single women have pushed dating to the bottom of their priority list. But, on some level, they still want and desire a fulfilling love relationship. As women, we naturally want to be happy in our relationships, but many of us don't know how. The rules of dating have changed, and most of us don't know what the new rules are. I believe that if you're going to take dating seriously in this hypercompetitive dating environment, you have no choice but to start to think differently and employ new strategies to attract the ideal man.

How You Live Your Single Life Is Key to Attracting the Love of Your Life

Women must first learn to be happy without a man. If you are unhappily single, we will seek to change that so you can get the most out of your single days. Being single should be one of the best times of your life. It is your time to discover what you want out of life, what your goals are, and what you need from a man. If you follow the strategies in this book, you will begin to enjoy your single life more.

I know you might be thinking that you don't want to enjoy being single; you want to get married. Well, if that is your end goal, you need to know that how you live as a single person determines the type of men you attract into your life. Having a full, productive single life is key to achieving a fulfilling committed relationship. If you are unhappy single, you will likely be unhappy married, except you can then blame your spouse instead of yourself for your unhappiness. Well, when you are living the life you want as a single woman, you will attract the man who is right for you.

If you are not enjoying dating, we will get you in dating shape mentally, physically and emotionally. You have to train yourself to focus clearly on your wants, needs and future goals. If you've ever been an athlete, you know that the key to success is *training and preparation*. Likewise, this book will help you with the training and preparation required to win the dating game. You will learn to date to have fun, not just to find a husband.

By following the strategies in this book, you will definitely increase your chances of finding a husband. However, if you date with "finding a husband" on your mind, you will likely miss much of the fun and enjoyment that dating brings. You will have to stop thinking that marriage is the ultimate goal. If marriages were so great, why are more than half of them ending in divorce? So, don't rush into marriage, take your time, enjoy dating, and choose the man who is best for you.

You Can Win the Dating Game

So what does it mean to "win the dating game"? It means that you will have to learn to get into the "game" and compete. Think of dating as a sport; you will have to practice dating until you take control of your dating life and achieve the results you desire. Just like an athlete trains and practices to compete and win, you will have to practice to begin to win the dating game.

If you think about it, most of us have never been taught how to date to find a compatible partner. There was no college course for it. Yes, many women have received advice from family or friends. We may have taken advice from other single women. But most of us are winging it as we go. There are some women who are obviously better at it than others. Well, have no fear; we will discuss the strategies that have worked for numerous other women.

They have worked for others and they can work for you. As I applied these strategies, my dating and relationship skills improved and I begin to achieve the results that I desired. I've been proposed to three times, engaged twice, and married once, and I've discovered that I simply love dating. I enjoy the process of dating and all the feelings associated with dating—the excitement, anticipation, anxiety, and newness of meeting new men. After reading this book, you will have a competitive advantage over other women if you apply these strategies.

How This Book Is Organized

Is your goal just to meet new men so you can have fun dating, or are you interested in a long-term committed relationship? Either way, this book is for you. *Why I Love Men* offers practical strategies that I have learned from friends, relatives and my own experiences. This book shares my experiences, various philosophies and some of the best practical advice that I have ever received and successfully applied. These ideas will help you identify and pursue the man who is right for you.

The book is divided into four parts:

1. *The Joys and Pains of Relationships.*

In this section, I share both my personal triumphs as well as my bad decisions in love and relationships. I share the heartfelt story of the joys and pains experienced in my relationships in a sister-to-sister, woman-to-woman, friend-to-friend manner. I believe that you will be able to relate to the stories and find them entertaining and encouraging; however, if you want to get right to the dating strategies and advice, begin in Part II.

2. *The Dating Action Plan: Become the Woman Every Man Wants.*

In this part, you learn the specific strategies that will help you become an exciting and highly desirable woman that men will want. I point out things that you may be doing wrong in your dating life and provide suggestions for approaches that work. You can't continue doing the same thing and expect different results. It is time to change your approach to dating!

3. *The Dating Action Plan: Find the Man that Every Woman Wants.*

In Part III, you will learn how to identify a mate who is right for you. It is important to understand that men think very differently than women about sex, dating and relationships. So you have to learn how men think in order to greatly increase your odds of finding a man.

4. *The Truths and Lessons Learned from Dating.*

In Part IV, I share the lessons learned and truths about men, love, dating and relationships. I will help you understand what men think, based upon what they have told me, as I have spent my entire life being around men. I'll reveal insights into the minds of men and uncover the secrets for attracting and keeping the men you want in your life. I had to learn these lessons the hard way, but I am now smarter and finally winning the dating game.

My book is designed to entertain, inform and completely transform your life. There are plenty of action items that will allow you to immediately begin to put these strategies into practice. Soon you'll start to get the positive results you desire!

For the next 30 days, select a different action item from the book each day. The goal is to begin to change your daily habits to move yourself toward creating the life you want and attracting love into your life.

I wish you the very best in getting the love you deserve.

PART I
THE JOYS AND PAINS
OF RELATIONSHIPS

THE JOYS AND PAINS
OF RELATIONSHIPS

Men have encouraged, supported and loved me my entire life. However, there are relationships with certain men that have significantly helped me to develop and grow into the woman I am today. In Part I, I share heartfelt stories of the joys and pains I've experienced over the years in my love relationships. I share both my personal triumphs as well as my bad decisions in love and relationships. After every bad decision, I've tried to use it to become wiser and smarter and to learn from it. My journey has taught me to be resilient and strong, never being afraid to make mistakes in life. The mistakes I've made have become my greatest learning and growth opportunities.

I believe I am successful in my relationships with men today because of the painful experiences that I had early in my dating life. I quickly learned what type of mistakes not to make again. I learned the lesson and used it to improve my next relationship. I vowed to be smarter and wiser about my approach with men going forward.

These stories are meant to encourage and inspire you in your own dating life. My hope is that you'll find the stories to be both engaging and entertaining, and that they will challenge you to live the incredible life you were born to live!

CHAPTER ONE

I Never Knew Eros (Sexual) Love Like This

I t was a Monday morning, and a time when my consulting career was continuing to be far more rewarding than I had ever expected. I planned to start a new project that day and was looking forward to the challenges that come with a new consulting assignment. On my way to work, I reflected on how pleased I was with my career as a Management Consultant. I loved the dynamic nature of consulting as I was working on various projects in different industries, with diverse clients. The work provided excitement and professional development opportunities, which enabled me to enjoy and excel in my career. I had received many awards, accolades and, most important, promotions and raises, and looked forward to future career opportunities.

As it relates to my career, I always wanted to be in control of my own destiny. There's nothing worse than hating your job, driving in a car you dislike, returning home to a neighborhood you don't like, and sleeping in a house that doesn't meet your expectations of a home. I felt great about avoiding all of those scenarios in my life.

And Then Came John Newman

As I walked into my new customer's building, I noticed that it was rather dark and quiet. I had been told that there weren't a lot of people who worked there and I even noticed that many of the offices were empty along the hallway. So I was hoping for an office all to myself and was disappointed to find that I would have an officemate while I worked there. I was also surprised to find that my new officemate was tall, dark and handsome, with a smile that lit up a room. He introduced himself as John Newman.

If I had to describe a picture of what my ideal mate was, he would have looked just like John. He shook my hand and looked at me like we were in a nightclub. The look seemed to say, "I'm going to hit that." But I didn't mind, I hadn't met many Black men in my field so working with him was bound to add more excitement to an already fulfilling career.

The first thing that comes to mind when I think of John is that he is the best liar I've ever met. Please understand me that when I say this guy was such a great liar, I mean he should have parlayed his skill for lying into a career! He was that skilled at lying, and it was a trait that I'd pay a price for later.

The next thing that comes to mind when I think of John is that he loved women. John had a knack for being intimate with women, not just physically, but emotionally as well. He was very fascinated by women and, most important, the sport of getting a woman. Plus, he loved women's bodies and, simply put, he understood more about the vagina than most females. Actually, not since I saw the play, *Vagina Monologues*, had I heard so many interesting stories about women and their vaginas. In fact, John should have written his own play. (A little side comment... I want to mention that going to the off-Broadway show, *Vagina*

Monologues, was one of the most empowering experiences I've had as a woman. It was a really powerful play. Every monologue relates to the vagina, whether it be through sex, love, rape, menstruation, mutilation, masturbation, birth or orgasm. One of the funniest stories was about the various names that are used to describe the vagina. Through it all, the main message of the show was that the vagina was a tool of female empowerment. This is a message that many women do not understand today.)

Throughout college, I had heard about porn movies, but until I met John, I had never seen one. John had a collection of them that he would watch and enjoy as if he was watching a movie or sitcom. I remember when we were living together (I'll explain later how that happened), I came home one day and John was watching a porn movie, but not just any porn movie. John took everything to another level. He was watching a 3D porn movie and was sitting there in the bedroom with 3D glasses on. I laughed so hard because he looked like a fool. I thought every guy watched porn movies in 3D. However, over the years, I found that not to be the case.

Since John and I shared an office, I got to know more and more about him every day. One thing that I learned about John was a clue not to get involved in a romantic relationship with him; this was the fact that he was always broke. However, he earned a very good income, even more than I made!

At the time we met, John was living with a woman about 10 years older than he was who obsessed over him. She apparently adored him; however, since John's divorce wasn't finalized from his wife (who still prayed for John to come back home to her and their two daughters), he wouldn't consider a serious committed relationship with the woman. I remember telling him that if you're living with a woman, whether you know it or not, you're already in a serious committed relationship.

John smoked, drank and gambled so much that it was hard to tell which one was his biggest vice. But at that time in my life, all of those things seemed trivial; and in fact, they made John even more intriguing to me. He was a bad boy.

One thing my grandma used to say was "It's good to live a sheltered life, that way you never have to find out what your vices are." Well, John introduced me to gambling. Let's just say that John took me to the casino and taught me blackjack, and I fell in love with it the first time I won a large "double down" bet. When I returned from my first casino trip, I decided to master blackjack. This was a great game for me because I had a college degree in mathematics and had a knack for numbers. I regularly studied blackjack, learned to count cards, and spent much of my free time in a casino. I think it's safe to say that blackjack became my vice.

Before I got really good at blackjack, I would lose lots of money. John and I would drive up to Atlantic City after work, and gamble all night, and then drive straight to work the next day (with no sleep). I remember one time we lost plenty of money and John had this bright idea to return the next day to win it back. But given the fact that John had lost all of our money the night before, I didn't know how this could be possible. John decided to take his company laptop to a pawn shop so we could use that money to win back the money we had already lost. And I actually thought this was a good idea! Thanks to God's grace and mercy, we won, and we were able to get his laptop back. If we hadn't won, and he couldn't retrieve his company's laptop, John would have likely lost his job. So, in some ways, we had no choice but to win, and we did.

I acquired so much skill at playing blackjack that eventually people would ask me to teach them how to play. In fact, a few years later, I taught a guy that I was dating how to play blackjack and he learned to maximize his blackjack play. One day after his skill level had significantly increased, we went to Atlantic City and my boyfriend said he needed to and planned to win $50,000. I replied, "Well, in that case, win about $10,000 for me." That seemed like such a ridiculous amount of money to try and win, but I soon realized that he wasn't joking. I helped him count cards and he had a focus that night that took all of the fun out of gambling. But when we left, he had won about $38,000. So I guess we both have John to thank for my blackjack skills. Even today, if I ever get in a bind, I know I could easily win $1-$2k with ease at any casino.

As John and I worked together every day in that small dark office, we became great friends. We started hanging out after work, during lunch, and eventually weekends. John and I became very close, but given that he still lived with his girlfriend, I didn't want to get involved with him.

John Moves in with Me

One morning John came into the office and said he and his girlfriend broke up and he needed a place to stay during his transition. I didn't hesitate to allow him to stay with me, because we were such great friends, and after all, friends help friends. I guess I was also secretly thinking that now John could be my guy. I thought this would be perfect, but it took less than two weeks before things started to blow up.

One day while we were both at work, the older woman (supposedly his ex-girlfriend) showed up at the job. The woman was furious because she didn't know where he had been for the last two weeks. Apparently, she didn't get the memo that they had broken up. I could tell she was really worried about him, and had no clue that he had "ended" the relationship. After this scene, John said that the woman was in denial, and that she knew they had broken up, but she was just crazy. So, from the very beginning of our relationship to the very end, there was always drama.

In the beginning, the drama was his ex-girlfriend showing up at the job frequently, calling him every hour during work, and constantly sending flowers to our office. Since I shared an office with him, I took offense to the fact that he put the flowers on his desk and enjoyed them, as well as all the attention of receiving flowers from her. One day John received the flowers, and as usual, he proudly placed them on his desk. As soon as he went to the bathroom, I took the flowers outside and threw them in the dumpster because I was so sick of the damn flowers. To this day, I hate to see people receive flowers at work.

As months went on, the drama continued. If it wasn't his ex-girlfriend, it was new women calling his cell phone all hours of the day and night. I knew this because I was both living and working with him, which created a living hell for me day and night.

Given all this drama with John, one would have to ask why in the world would any woman want to deal with this man. Quite frankly, the sex was the best I've ever experienced in my life. So this caused me to accept circumstances that I just wouldn't imagine that I would tolerate. Since my book isn't a "sexy urban novel," I will spare you the details. But let me just say that John was a perfect lover and the worst boyfriend I've ever had. Throughout this relationship of one year (yes, John ended up staying with me for nearly a year), I never felt more insecure and inadequate in my life. In fact, because of John, I know the pain of infidelity because I have experienced it. The pain that won't allow you to sleep because your boyfriend said he was going to call or come by at a specific time and the sun has risen and there's still been no word from him. John would get home around 5 and 6 in the morning after "hanging out with his guy friends." I don't know of any club that is open until that hour. But John always had a good excuse, with supportable evidence and friends to vouch for him. I could never catch him in a lie, but I always knew that he was lying to me. A woman's intuition is typically right.

The Break-Up

One day, John and I had plans to go see a movie after work. I remember this so vividly because it was a Will Smith movie that I had been waiting weeks to see. As we were about to leave work, John told me to go ahead and return home alone because he needed to work late. I asked how he would get home and John said he could catch a ride. I thought to myself, "Let the lies begin!"

When John arrived home that evening, he indicated that he and some of his guy friends were planning a weekend ski trip... and leaving that night. I asked, "How could you have a ski trip planned when I never heard about it until now?" John said, "The other guys already had everything planned, and originally I didn't want to go... but they talked me into it." I sat on the bed and thought to myself that as of that day, I would accept no more lies from John. I also thought that when John left, I would cut up all his clothes while he was away. But then I thought that would be childish, especially if John really was on a ski trip. I then got a better idea. Since John's cell phone rang like a telethon hotline, I thought I'd somehow try to get his voicemail code and see where he was really going for the weekend.

As John started gathering his clothes for the weekend, his phone continued to ring, and as usual, he let his phone go to voicemail. I discreetly followed him to every room in the house, because I was determined to get his voicemail code when he checked his messages. Finally, he pulled the phone out of his pocket. I turned my back to pretend I wasn't looking, but I looked out the corner of my eye, and quickly memorized the code number. As John packed his bags, I ignored him the entire time because I was focused on when I would get an opportunity to check his voicemail messages. And the chance arrived when John went to take a shower. I picked up his cell phone, dialed his voicemail, and began listening to his voicemail messages. There were romantic messages from two different women who I didn't know and then the ex-girlfriend (the older woman) had left a message confirming what time they were going on a ski trip to celebrate their anniversary. I was sick to my stomach. I finally realized that the entire time we were together, he had continued to see his ex-girlfriend. As I sat there, I was too hurt to even be mad. In fact, I was devastated and very sad. In my heart, I knew then that all the drama would come to an end that night.

When John came out of the shower, I asked him where he was going for the weekend. I was surprised to find that he told me the city, the state and which guy friends were going. Even after hearing the voicemail from his ex-girlfriend, it sounded really believable.

After John walked out the door, I tried to decide what my next move would be. I couldn't think clearly and started to cry and apparently fell asleep. When I woke up, it was about 9 p.m. and I really needed evidence to bring closure to the relationship. I decided to go to his ex-girlfriend's house and see if his truck was there. I remember that when I woke up I had on purple plaid pajamas and purple slippers, and I thought to myself that since I'm already dressed I might as well go and get my evidence. It never dawned on me to put real clothes on because it really didn't matter what I had on, as I was on a mission.

I was so angry while driving down Constitution Avenue in Washington, DC that I never really noticed any of the stoplights. However, after about the third or fourth light, apparently one turned red. I ran that red light and hit a black car in the intersection. I would soon come to find out that this was not just any black car.

As I sat in my car in disbelief, I looked down at my clothes and thought, What am I doing out looking like this? Still sitting behind the steering wheel, I soon noticed that not only did one police car arrive, but there were about 20 police cars that had surrounded me. I wondered about so many police cars being there, and I would soon learn why.

A gentleman in a black suit came over to the car and said, "Ma'am, please get out of the car." I said, "Sure," because how much worse could this get? As I got out of the car, a policeman came over and stared at my attire and my hair (which was a hot mess) and said, "Ma'am, are you ok?" For some reason, I just rolled my eyes at him and refused to answer. He told me that I had hit a car in the President's security detail/entourage and they needed to investigate me. I replied, "You have got to be kidding me." Soon another police officer came over, and asked what happened. He also wanted to know if I needed a coat or jacket to put on. I rolled my eyes at him too and said, "I'm dressed, thank you."

I then called the one person who I knew would understand my situation and that is my best friend, Barbara. Everyone needs to have a true best friend, that person who never judges and is always supportive of both the good and the bad in your life. *This is Barbara.* I also knew that she was the only person who could make me feel better about this situation.

Because of what I hit, it must have taken three hours before I was cleared to leave. I had to leave with Barbara because my car wasn't even drivable. As we left the scene of the accident, I asked Barbara if there was a chance that we could still drive by John's ex-girlfriend's house to see if his truck was there and she said, "Hell no!" She told me that I got the evidence I needed through his voicemail, and didn't need any more; it was time to move on.

Barbara proved to be right; that was the last night I dealt with John. She took me home and helped me pack up his things. As I balled up his clothes and threw them in the trash bag, she would go behind me and neatly fold them. She kept saying, "You don't want to let him have the satisfaction of knowing how angry you are." After we packed up John's clothes, we also decided to go see that Will Smith movie because when I awoke that morning, that's all I had hoped for that day—none of the drama, lying, stealing voicemail codes, hitting cars. I just wanted to go see the Will Smith movie. I enjoyed the movie and started to prepare my mind for the pain and recovery that was to come.

When John returned on Sunday night, I told him to take his things (which thanks to my best friend were all neatly packed in a bag) and to go back to his ex-girlfriend's house. John said, "What are you talking about? Is that where you thought I was?" He added, "You can call one of my boys and they will tell you that I was with them." I answered, "I have no doubt that they will, but it really doesn't matter now." He continued to come up with more creative lies, but I wasn't even listening. I just stared at the TV, for I was done with that relationship. My grandma used to say, "Don't try to hold on to things that God is trying to take out of your life; just let them go." So I just let go.

As you could imagine, work was awkward, but over the next few weeks, John and I remained cordial and friendly. After all, men will only do what you allow them to do, so I had no one to blame but myself. From the first day I met him, John had showed me who he was, and when people

13

show you who they are, always believe them the first time. I knew who John was and what he was about and I deserved better than what he had to offer.

After the break-up, I would think about that relationship and sense that there was something different that I felt about this guy, but I couldn't quite understand it. I honestly could say that I loved him and hated him, sometimes even in the same day. Although I didn't understand it while I was in the relationship, I knew that the love I had for him was very powerful, but not of God. I had to explore and dig deeper and I asked God to lead me to an understanding so I could have peace again.

As I reflected on the relationship, I sat down one Saturday afternoon to read the Bible. I feel that God begin to reveal something to me through the Scriptures and it really blessed my heart by giving me a better sense of understanding of my situation. I began to understand much more about love and the types of love. I went online to continue studying and have been blessed to this day by what I learned.

Understanding the Three Types of Love: Eros, Philos and Agape

Through self-study and exploration, I learned that there are three types of love: *Eros, Philos* and *Agape*. I had never known that before, but understanding this concept has been enlightening for me. Here's what I learned:

Eros Love: The English word "erotic" is derived from Eros, and it has to do with the sensual passions. It is not found in Biblical usage. Eros love is also known as romantic or emotional love, and it constitutes the feeling of being "in love." This love is best expressed through our senses—touch, sight, hearing, etc. Eros is similar to lust, which is that intense sexual desire or overwhelming longing or craving for someone. Eros or lust is generally hormonally driven. Estrogen and testosterone are the hormones that work like magnets to draw men and women together. Eros love is good in a relationship if it is balanced with the other two loves because it allows for intimate sexual relations with someone and keeps the flame and spark in the relationship. Eros love may be the number one illusion for single women.

Philos Love: This type of love is the natural affection between people. Philos love is about companionship and connecting with people to share life's journey. It is sometimes called "friendship love," and friendship is the foundation of a successful relationship. This is true whether it is a marriage, or boyfriend-girlfriend, a relationship between family members, a relationship with co-workers, an employer, etc.

Agape Love: This type of love is from God, and it is an unconditional love. Agape love is above Philos and Eros love. It is a love that is totally selfless; like when a person gives love to another person even if this act does not benefit her/him in any way. Whether the love given is returned or not, the person continues to love (even without any self-benefit). This type of love provides the stability and binding commitment to a marriage. Agape love helps bind the marriage commitment because you vow to love your spouse as God loves—unconditionally. Agape love is not helped by emotional infatuation or highs, but is as constant as God's love.

All three types of love are necessary in a marriage or committed romantic relationship. Agape love (unconditional love) helps make the marriage commitment last, Philos love (friendship love) will make it strong, and Eros love (emotional/erotic love) will make it sweet. If your marriage or relationship has all three of these elements, you're on your way to something very special and rare that you should treasure with all that is in you.

Understanding the Effect Sex Has on Our Relationships

Many of us don't understand the effect sex has on our relationships. As women, we have to be extremely careful of who we have sex with. I date a lot but have very few sexual relationships. When a woman has sex with a man, hormones are released into her body that create a chemical bond, regardless of whether she wants that bond or not. This may be why many women feel conflicted emotionally when they have sex with a guy; there has been a bond that was created through the sex act.

When you have sex with someone, your soul becomes one with them. My grandma used to say that every time we have sex with someone in our bed, their spirit stays there. Likewise, when you end an intimate relationship with someone, it takes time to recover who we really are because we lose a part of ourselves in the other person. We have to spend quality time with ourselves to recapture who we really are.

Recovering from Eros Love

If you've found yourself in a primarily Eros love relationship, don't worry. Realize that this relationship has provided an opportunity for you to learn and grow so that you can attract the right man who will offer you a higher type of love. The unfortunate reality is that some women don't want to grow; they just want a man, at any cost. As a result, women end up repeating a cycle of unsuccessful relationships.

My best sexual relationship ever (with John) was also my toughest relationship to get out of and the same relationship that took me away from who I really was as a person. I came out of the relationship with John and focused on strengthening my relationship with God. I began my journey by deciding to be celibate for over two years. For me, celibacy was more than abstaining from sexual intercourse; it was also about abstaining from any type of deeply committed relationship. During this time of celibacy, I was able to devote time and energy to focus on my spiritual growth and development.

Now I am grateful that my Eros love led me to my deepest, most fulfilling relationship with God and helped me understand Agape love and its powerful presence in my life.

CHAPTER TWO

Why I'm a S&M (Success and Money) Diva

My focus on career took hold when I began my first job at a prestigious management consulting firm. I can honestly say consulting has proven to be an enjoyable and lucrative career choice. On my first day, I was simply happy to have landed such a great job right out of college, but I didn't have any particular career aspirations or goals at that time. However, the focus on achieving career success started the day I heard Jared Ashton give a speech. In fact, Jared inspired me throughout the first 10 years of my career. He was my model of corporate success. Jared was brilliant, an amazing communicator, and well-respected by everyone in the company. He was a tall dark-skinned Black guy, and one of the most masculine men I had encountered in some time. Jared had been a partner in the firm for many years, and he exuded self-confidence to the point that I felt nervous and shy around him. I later discovered that even some of his peers felt that way around him, too.

From the first day I saw Jared, I was immediately attracted to his success. I realized that success, power and money are desirable traits in a man. And he had all of them. It didn't matter that he never gave me the time of day; it only matter that he existed. In my college days I had heard about the challenges experienced by Blacks in the workplace. But from the moment I came across Jared, I knew that achieving great success in Corporate America was possible.

The first day I arrived at the management consulting firm, I was told about the two African American partners. There were only two Blacks that held such coveted positions and every Black person at the firm knew of them. Yet, most, including myself, had not met or seen them. However, during my first month with the company, Jared Ashton was scheduled to speak at a town hall meeting in Washington, DC to discuss career paths and opportunities. I couldn't wait to attend this meeting, and many other African Americans felt the same way. I dressed in my best corporate suit, had my hair freshly permed, and made sure my makeup was perfect. On my way to the town hall meeting, I actually felt nervous, but at that time I was not certain as to why. It felt almost like a first date. I can now admit that I had a huge crush on Jared Ashton.

At the event, I learned that Jared would be the first and only speaker, which made perfect sense. He is such a powerful and dynamic speaker, no one could possibly follow him. He spoke of the skills required to be a great consultant and advance at the firm. However, he felt that there was no secret knowledge or skills required because we were African American. Once Jared finished speaking, he came out into the crowd to mingle, and he was literally swarmed by people wanting to speak to him. I thought there is no way I'd get an opportunity to meet him. So I just left and kept him as the picture of success in my mind.

My Plan to Work with Jared

Since Jared was based in New York, and I was out of the DC Metro Area, it would be several months before I'd have an opportunity to see him again. In the meantime, I knew that the only way I'd get to spend any time with him would be to accelerate my career advancement at the firm. Since Jared was a partner, and I was a junior consultant, the likelihood of us working closely together wouldn't be likely, unless I proved myself to be of more value to the company. I thought that if I became his peer or reached a senior enough level, I'd get to work with him on an assignment.

So, one Friday night, after a long day, I went and purchased numerous books on management consulting, career advancement, and general professional development. After studying the books, I laid out my action plan of what I needed to do to advance my career, but I thought it also made sense to solicit feedback from my manager. I set up a meeting with my manager for Monday morning to get his input on my development needs. During that meeting, I learned that there were a lot more development opportunities that I would have to work on if I stood any chance of being promoted. The most important feedback that my manager provided at that time shocked me. To this day, I have never forgotten it. He said, "You're very bright, but you do not communicate well. If you cannot communicate your ideas as a consultant, it's the same as if you had no ideas. As consultants, we are constantly selling ideas and solutions and your ability to communicate this will make or break your success." I thought to myself, I didn't expect this, but it was really good to know. Other areas of improvement included developing industry expertise in a particular technology or discipline and to dress for the role I hoped to attain, not the one I was currently in. This was all great information, and I had enough feedback to develop an action plan.

The improvement in my communication skills has been a great asset to me in both my personal and professional life. I spent weeks with a speech therapist to improve my diction, enunciation and tone. Apparently, I didn't articulate well enough nor did I have polish in my communication style. My speech consultant taught me about everything ranging from enunciation, diction, breathiness, tone, pace and articulation. Week after week, this training transformed my voice more and more into a powerful tool for communicating my ideas. The next area of training focused on presentation and facilitation skills. I took a five-day training course that taught me to be a dynamic speaker and learned how to facilitate meetings so that they would be purposeful and on track, with action items and outcomes achieved. Today I look at every conversation that I have with a potential mate as a "presentation" of who I am. After all this training, which was paid for by the firm, they wasted no time putting it to good use. I was obviously doing well and gaining the confidence of management because I was quickly thrown in to leading meetings and conducting presentations to customers. In just one year, I received numerous performance awards and a promotion, which made me feel confident that I was on track with my grand plan: to advance in my career, and become a peer of Jared Ashton so that I could work more closely with him. Of course, the end goal didn't have to be a romantic relationship with Jared, but that would be the best case scenario. I knew that even if this didn't happen, just having him as a mentor and friend would significantly improve the quality of my work life.

My First Opportunity to Work with Jared

After my first year at the firm, I was selected as an African American high achiever. This afforded me the opportunity to participate in a Diversity Initiative that focused on improving the career advancement opportunities for minorities. That was a huge accomplishment, as the only people on the committee were partners, the Diversity Director and me. I was selected to represent the voice of the "up and coming" minorities with great potential for career advancement at the firm. All this was great, but here's the thing that really mattered to me: Jared Ashton was a member of this Diversity committee, and I was going to be in monthly meetings with him in New York City. I was so excited to see my grand plan starting to work.

At the first meeting, I was so nervous because my muse was going to be in the meeting. As I arrived, I felt beyond nervous and wasn't sure what I would say. So, when Jared came in, I just said, "Hello, how are you?" Jared glanced at me as he fixed his plate from the catered breakfast that was placed out for us, and said, "Fine." Then he turned and walked away, as if I didn't even exist. He obviously didn't know how important this meeting was to me. Even though Jared never communicated directly to me during the entire meeting, I noticed that something really significant was happening. I realized there were many powerful commu-

nication styles in the room. I mean beyond the basic communication and enunciation strategies that I had learned.
The partners were brilliant communicators, all very pre-
cise, colorful and impactful, and some were even funny. I
had never seen anything like it, but I knew that they were
communicating at a level that was beyond anything I had
ever heard or experienced.

So, after I took my flight home that night, I went
straight to the bookstore again to learn about these powerful communication styles that I had heard earlier in the day.
I found a book that I recommend to all consultants on my
team today. It is called *I Wish I'd Said That!* by Linda
McCallister. It discusses the various communication styles
and their effectiveness, as well as how to best communicate
with people based upon their communication style. As I
went through the book, I matched a partner name with
every one of the communication styles. I even found my
own communication style and was able to hone it based
upon the suggestions in the book. This book helped me
truly understand the power of communication and its
either positive or negative effect on the listener. This
became a lesson that was a valuable asset throughout my
consulting career and personal life.

I'd like to tell you that as a result of these monthly
Diversity meetings, I got to know or grew close to Jared.
Unfortunately, I never even got to have a conversation with
him. I don't think he purposely ignored me, I just never
made his radar. In fact, to this day, we have never had a
conversation even though, over the years, we ended up in
several meetings together. I knew Jared always recognized
me but I don't think he ever knew my name. If I saw him

in the hall, Jared would speak because I looked familiar to him, but he would never say my name and we all know this generally means that the person doesn't know your name.

So, after about 10 years of trying to become the best consultant I could be so that I would befriend Jared, I left that management consulting firm. This work ethic and discipline that I acquired over my 10 years at the firm has stayed with me throughout my career. After leaving the firm, I've had many career achievements such as running my own consulting firm for about four years. I also became Vice President of Technical Operations in a large Fortune 500 company in the Northeast and was the youngest African American to receive a Vice President position at that company by the age of 32.

I've had many mentors in my career over the years, but I have looked at Jared Ashton as my main role model for corporate success. I even followed his career through articles about his successes and accomplishments because I was deeply proud of him. Even though I did not get to know him personally, I am so appreciative of the contributions he made to my career. Today I owe a lot of my career success to a man named Jared Ashton.

And Then Came Along Materialistic Sam

During the 10 years at the managing consulting firm, I only had one or two boyfriends because I focused so much time on my career. I didn't get involved in any serious relationships until after I started my own IT consulting firm. Investing in my career didn't leave much time for dating.

Once I started my firm, I earned a significant income, bought my first home, and was investing in a 401k plan.

And at the time in my life when I was the strongest financially, I met materialistic Sam. I have to pause before I begin this story, because Sam was the only man that I ever let mess with my money. And, boy, did he really mess with my money!

Sam was a military guy who had a steady income and good benefits, and he was always dressed sharply and offered a great friendly smile. I met him at a new church I was attending and thought it was refreshing to meet such a great guy in church. One important thing to mention about Sam was that he was extremely materialistic. When we met, he had a rimmed up SUV with TVs in the headrest. If he had a TV at home, it had to be a top-of-the-line plasma TV. If he had a watch, it would be a Rolex. He loved fine things.

Despite this, Sam and I hit it off right away. I felt comfortable with him because we spent so much time together pursuing our relationship with God and learning and growing spiritually. I felt so comfortable with Sam that I took him to meet my mom within the first two weeks of knowing him and she liked him right away.

At the time when I met Sam, I was traveling a lot as a result of my flourishing consulting business. I was making more money than I ever targeted in my career goals. I had savings and a brand new Mercedes-Benz S class sedan. After Sam and I had been dating for two years, he had the bright idea that we should merge our bank accounts. He so graciously offered to pay both his and my bills every month to make it easier for me, since I traveled so frequently.

Our relationship was great for me. We got along well,

particularly since I only saw Sam every other weekend. With all the traveling, I didn't have to be too involved emotionally with Sam, which was perfect for me. There were some days when I didn't want to speak to Sam because I always felt single and enjoyed my freedom. I think Sam noticed this, and he would express some concern if I didn't talk to him for days because he wanted to maintain the relationship and the great financial situation "we" had attained. I remember coming home from business trips and finding new gadgets in my house. There would be new flat screen TVs, new grills, and new furniture. You name it and he bought it. Meanwhile, the fact that I had a poor relationship with money caused this excessive spending to be of little concern to me. I always thought money was for spending and not saving.

The Engagement

After two years of dating, Sam proposed, and I said yes. He bought me a huge 3 carat diamond ring, which was great, except that it came out of our "joint" account. I remember being happy to be engaged, but really hesitant about doing any real wedding planning. In fact, we were engaged but I refused to discuss any wedding dates. For me, the relationship felt comfortable but it was no longer growing. I believed that anything that was not growing is dead. Then the wonderful church where we met had a 12 week pre-marital class that was spoken of highly by all who attended. I suggested that Sam and I attend the class. Sam had no objection, so I enrolled us.

This pre-marital class was one of the most impactful experiences that I've had in my life. It was designed to help couples determine if they were compatible and emotionally ready to move forward with marriage. It also covered what to expect of marriage. During this class, I learned with certainty that my fiancé and I should not get married. In fact, this class started with about 28 couples, and by Week 10, there were only about eight couples left. I think the class was very effective at helping couples avoid getting married at the wrong time or for the wrong reasons.

This class taught me more about me than I ever expected. There were personality and compatibility inventories and surveys that help me learn about my personality traits, what I emotionally and physically needed from a mate, and what marriage meant to me. Over the 12 weeks, we covered many important topics ranging from money, sex, roles, religious beliefs, child-rearing, extended family, and other areas that commonly cause marriages to fail and lead to divorce. During one session, we were asked to bring our financial information, such as checking/savings account information, credit card debt, credit scores, etc. so that we could share it with each other. About half the class dropped out during this session because they refused to share their financial information with their mate. We learned that many couples were comfortable having sex with each other, but when it came to their finances, they were not willing to share as easily.

Another valuable exercise was a homework assignment called "Questions to Ask before You Say I Do." They recommended that we go to a nice quiet restaurant and answer the questions over dinner. These questions were so thought-provoking that I thought I'd share a few of them with you:

- Describe your spiritual journey and relationship with God over the last 10 years.

- If I were a doctor who was describing your medical history, what would it include (including accidents, STDs, hospital stays, etc.)?

- Where do you see yourself in 10 years (financially, emotionally, spiritually, family size)?

- What are three habits that you wish you didn't have and what are three habits that you are glad you have?

- What people in your life have influenced you the most and in what way?

- Why did your last serious relationship end?

- What was the most difficult thing that's ever happened to you in life?

- Do you want children? If so, how many?

- What are your financial responsibilities and obligations, including debt, child support, etc.?

- Who are the people in your life who you need to forgive or apologize to and for what reason?

I wanted to share these questions in case anyone reading this book may not get the opportunity to attend a formal pre-marital class. Even if you're not planning to get married or are not even dating someone, I would encourage you to answer these questions for yourself. They'll help you better understand who you are and how you arrived at this point in your life.

The pre-marital class confirmed that the man I was planning to marry was the wrong guy. This revelation happened in the Week 10 class. Our assignment was to write down 10 characteristics of our ideal mate, including their physical, spiritual and personality traits. Once we created our list, we were to fold the list and seal it in an envelope. Given that we put this information in a sealed envelope, no one ever thought that our partners would ever see the list. However, at the end of the class, we were asked to exchange envelopes and share this information with our mates. This is where it all went bad for Sam and me. My fiancé's list reflected a lot of who I was. However, my list did not reflect any characteristics of my fiancé—not a single one! I wanted a man who was ambitious, with a sense of self-confidence, piercing intelligence, etc. I realized then that it didn't make sense to marry a man who didn't have any of the characteristics and traits that I was looking for in my ideal mate. I wondered how I ended up engaged to someone who did not line up with what I wanted in a partner. So many times women let the man choose her, but it's time we start choosing what is best for us.

At that moment, I knew that if I married Sam, I would be making the biggest mistake of my life. Although we finished the class, I broke off the engagement shortly afterwards and ended the relationship. It was painful to know that the person I loved and planned to marry was all wrong for me.

The Break-Up

The break-up was not that difficult for me because I traveled most of the week and wasn't used to seeing Sam that often, about every other weekend. After a few months, I took a consulting assignment that would be in New York City for several months, and because NYC is one of my favorite places in the world, I soon decided to get a place in Weehawken, New Jersey and stay a few years. I was enjoying NYC and my "sex in the city" experiences, and appreciated all the fashion, nightlife and food that the city had to offer. My absolute favorite thing to do was to go to Broadway shows. New York was really enjoyable at a time when I really needed to press forward in life.

In all the hecticness of my new and exciting life, I realized that it made more sense to sell my house since I had an apartment in Weehawken and spent the majority of my time in NYC. The relationship with Sam was still cordial and, in fact, he still stayed at my house from time to time. So, as long as Sam had access to my house and money (because I hadn't found the time to get a separate checking account), he never was difficult around my decision to call off the engagement. One day, during a conversation, Sam was kind enough to offer to assist me with the sale of my house. Sam told me that if I gave him Power of Attorney, he could oversee the sale of the house. Unfortunately, I didn't fully understand what it meant to give someone Power of Attorney, but I trusted him; after all, he was my former fiancé.

The last time I remember speaking to Sam was to discuss the details of the upcoming sale of the house. On the day of the sale, I remember that I couldn't reach him in the morning. In fact, I couldn't reach him at all during or after the sale of my house. Because he had Power of Attorney, Sam was able to keep all of the proceeds from the house and I never heard from him again. This was devastating, and after researching the transaction, I found out that the proceeds from the house were about $80,000. Sam kept it all and never contacted me again.

I wish I could say that this is where the story ends, as if that's not bad enough. I honestly could not find Sam nor did any of his phone numbers work. A year earlier Sam retired from the military, and he had been spending most of his time taking classes preparing for a new career. Well, this story gets worse. When I went to purchase another home, that is when the bomb dropped. I was told that I may not be able to get the house because my credit scores were too low. By too low, I mean that my scores ranged from about 560 to 620 but I knew I hadn't had any major credit issues or missed payments. When the lender showed me my credit report, I saw that Sam had co-signed me to $40,000 in credit card loans, a $50,000 debt consolidation loan, and a new $60,000 Cadillac. This totally blew my mind. None of these items were mine, but they all appeared on my credit report and were drastically weighing down my credit score. I wasn't upset at this time, I was mad as hell!

I decided that the best thing for me to do was to fight back. After several months of lawyers and courts, I was able to get both the $50,000 debt consolidation loan and the $60,000 Cadillac off my credit report because they had no proof of signatures from me for these loans. I was not so lucky with the credit card loans. Apparently, Sam had gotten those two credit cards when we still had a joint account together and the lender had evidence that I had used one of the credit cards for a purchase. So I got stuck with the $40,000 of credit card debt that did not belong to me. I never shared this with my family because I know my male cousins (Pooky and others) would spend every waking moment trying to find Sam and I didn't want any of them going to jail on my account.

The Search for Sam

I remember that for years after we broke up, I always wanted to find Sam. I had a few things I wanted to say but no one, including my attorney, could find this guy. But because the desire to find him still existed for me, I was always on the lookout for clues to locate Sam. Then one day, to my excitement, I finally came across some information on his whereabouts.

On that day, I checked my credit report (which I do monthly now), and it indicated that I had a new address in Cincinnati, Ohio. Well, I knew this wasn't my address. I figured that it must be Sam's address because his sisters and brothers all lived in Cincinnati, and he always wanted to live there as well. Because our finances were so intertwined and he had co-signed me on those loans as his spouse, when he moved, my credit report was updated with his new address.

So I wrote down this address, but wasn't sure what to do with it. One option was to call my cousin Pooky and then drive with him to Cincinnati to visit Sam. However, I didn't want to end up on the news. I really only wanted to speak with Sam to understand why he would try to steal my money and ruin my credit. At least I thought that's what I wanted to do. However, I held that address for months. During that time, I looked at it so much that I even had it memorized.

One day, I received an opportunity to take a consulting assignment in Cincinnati, Ohio, and I would need to be onsite with the customer for about two months. You wouldn't believe how quickly I jumped at the opportunity to take this assignment. My first thought was I am definitely going to pay Sam an unexpected visit when I arrive to Cincinnati!

As my plane landed in Ohio, it was Sunday evening and still light out. I knew I would have time to go find Sam at the address that I had obtained a few months earlier. So, after I got a rental car with a navigational system, I headed straight to the address.

Much to my surprise, as I was driving to the address, I noticed that the neighborhood was getting worse and worse with every mile that I passed. I then started seeing liquor stores, beauty supply stores, and cash checking centers on every block. I didn't have a good feeling about the unexpected visit that I was planning to make.

Eventually, I arrived to the address that I had kept in my wallet for so many months. What I saw was shocking. It was a run-down house, in desperate need of a paint job, with a broken screen door. Still I assumed Sam was in there because his rimmed out Cadillac Escalade, that I had to fight so long to get off my credit report, was parked to the side of the house.

I parked on the street as I was deciding whether I would actually go to the door and knock. But I was thinking, after I knock, then what? I figured that this could get ugly and I didn't have any of my cousins around to back me up. So I did the only thing I know to do when I get myself into dicey situations and that was to pray. I had so much I wanted to say to this guy, but what good could come out of this encounter? After I prayed, I felt that God had spoken to me. I believed that God's message to me was: "Everything he has taken from you, I have returned to you in great abundance." At that moment, I fully understood the meaning of the song, "What God Has for Me, It Is for Me." This guy or no other man can take my blessings, whether they are spiritual, physical or financial; what God has for me, it is for me. At that point, I decided to drive to my hotel room and enjoy my evening.

When I arrived at the hotel, to reinforce the message I had just received from God, I was given the largest suite in the hotel. Due to my platinum status as a frequent traveler, the hotel clerk said that I qualified for an upgraded suite. He told me it was my lucky day because the only suite they had available was the presidential suite, the largest suite in the hotel, which had been occupied by actual presidents over the years. Having been upgraded to suites in the past, I didn't think too much of this comment. However, when I walked upstairs to my room, I noticed the suite was so large that it had several doors for the entry. When I walked in, I was amazed. The hotel suite was about 1200 square feet, with a living room, kitchen, den, two bedrooms and a Jacuzzi tub. It occupied the entire corner of the hotel! I felt incredibly blessed and made sure to enjoy the room as it had been a very emotional day. I never felt the need to return to Sam's address during my stay in Cincinnati, and I never tried to look him up again.

I was not able to buy my second house around that time due to my credit challenges. However, a few years later, after I had rebuilt my credit, I did purchase a new home in a great neighborhood. It actually took several years to rebuild my credit, and as a result, to this day, I check my credit report every month to ensure there is no erroneous information on it. I use credit watch services as well so that I will know when there is a change to my credit. As a result of this, I truly know and appreciate the value of a good credit score.

Through it all, I have learned to never let a man mess with my money again. I vowed to never let that happen again. I worked so hard to achieve my career goals and earn an income beyond what I had planned, only to see the fruits of my labor stomped on. To this day, I will never let a man drag me down financially. He has to bring some-thing to the table or he is not welcome in my life. My aunt always said, "I can do bad by myself, I don't need any help to starve to death."

CHAPTER THREE

Reaching My Beauty Potential

When I was in high school, I could never get a date. I grew up with about five female cousins who were all my age and all beautiful. Now that I look back, I understand why I could never get a date. I had thick "soda bottle" glasses, and was a size 0 with no hairstyle. Being slim may have been a good thing, but being a size 0 has never been cool. My hair looked like I was still in elementary school with large bangs and a mushroom style in the back.

During high school, I barely made it to the prom my senior year. I wasn't as lucky as my cousins who got asked to the prom for their sophomore, junior and senior years. However, one of my cousins offered to go on a date with a guy if he would take me to my senior prom. As a result, he decided to take me to the prom and I didn't mind; I guess a date who had been bribed was better than no date at all!

Not having guys interested in me in high school was a problem; however, I chose to focus on making good grades. I figured that my academic achievements made my parents proud, and I would have time to date after I graduated high school.

I remember having discussions with my grandma and I told her, "No guys like me, and they all think I'm ugly." My grandma said, "No worries… God gave you a beauty mark on your face, so he's already stamped you as beautiful regardless of what those guys think." Since my grandma was full of wisdom and generally right about everything, I assumed she was right about this and all those guys were just wrong about not liking me.

On the other hand, my brothers did their part to mock my appearance. Still, that is how we bantered with each other, so it was all in fun. One of my brothers called me "Big Eye, Little Eye" to make fun of my lazy eye. I had eye surgery when I was about five years old, and as a result, one of my eyes was slightly smaller than the other. But I also had my share of nicknames for my brothers. While we always teased each other for fun, I knew they had my back at all times.

Since high school, I have always been sensitive about my appearance, to say the least. However, I didn't think a person had many options when it came to their looks and appearance. I would later find out how wrong I was.

Very Few Dates in College

My dating woes continued when I went to college, which made sense because I had the same tired look which had never caught the attention of guys in high school. However, I still wasn't too concerned about my appearance; since I had made straight A's in high school, I planned to continue that same focus on academics in college. Up to this point, my claim to fame in life was my academic success, and those achievements came with several awards and paid tuition for scholastic achievements. My academic success remained the most important thing to me.

During college, I continued making great grades, had several wonderful friends, and enjoyed hanging out from time to time. My friends were fly girls from New York and the DC Metro area. Not only were these ladies cute, but they had plenty of fashion and style and knew how to work it to their advantage. I always admired them for that, and knew that these ladies were in a league all by themselves.

When I was in my early 20s after I graduated from college, I began to date more frequently and focus on my personal life. I met a lot of nice guys, but no one really special. However, there was one date that I went on that changed my dating experiences forever. While on a dinner date with a guy that I had met at the mall, I remember him being very disinterested and distracted during the dinner. I asked him what was wrong and he indicated that he was fine, just tired from work. I then asked him what type of women that he typically dated, and he said, without hesitation, "Normally gorgeous women, but you seemed so cool when we talked on the phone, so I thought you'd be cool to hang out with." This was very direct, but I realized that he wasn't actually trying to be insensitive, so maybe he had more to share with me. I said, "What do you think about me?" He replied, "You're not that attractive, but you have potential." This comment struck a chord with me because I knew this guy was being sincere, albeit insensitive, so I just took it as constructive criticism. I kept thinking, What did he mean when he said I had 'potential'? I thought, Potential to become what?

I didn't get a second date with this guy because he said I wasn't his type. However, I still had his phone number. After a couple of weeks, I called him because I was curious about his "potential" comment. When he picked up the phone, I said, "This is Jennifer, how are you?" He said, "Who?" I had to give him the details of who I was, where we went to eat, etc. (Don't you hate it when a guy acts like he doesn't remember who you are?) Once he remembered me, I asked him, "What did you mean when you said I had potential?" He said, "You could be fine if you wanted to because you have all the requisite skills; with a little work, you could be really attractive." I replied, "Can you be more specific?" He told me, "If you got rid of your acne, did something with your hair, and wore some clothes to show off your body, you would be quite attractive. You would look so much better if you just put some effort into your appearance. Right now, it is clear that you could care less about how you look." I told him that I did care about it, and that my clothes were always clean, pressed and presentable. He said, "Yes, but you are not appealing to men." Because I had to be pretty thick-skinned growing up with all brothers, I continued to take his input as constructive criticism. I thanked him for his feedback and let the guy get back to his evening.

My Beauty Transformation

Now I had to think about what I was going to do with this feedback. I decided to give "making an effort" a try. I would "work" at improving my appearance so that I could be more attractive to men. I began my plans to begin my transformation and reach my beauty *potential*. I transformed myself with a total focus on outward beauty. And it really made a difference in how much I was able to attract men and create a fun dating life. On this note, a great Essence book that discusses ways to keep your hair, skin and body beautiful is called *Beauty Basics and Beyond* by Patricia M. Hinds.

I believe that you need to do several beauty transformations over your lifetime, because it's easy to get distracted by other things after a while. I've done two beauty transformations. The first was that time back in my 20s that I was just discussing. My recent transformation occurred about a year ago after coming out of a period of focusing on my work and career. Here are the before and after photos related to my more recent transformation.

Before   *After*

As you'll see below, a beauty transformation focuses on techniques that anyone can do to maximize their physical beauty, with no cosmetic surgery. Here is a list of the steps you'll want to take; they come from my second beauty transformation:

Seek professional advice from a personal image consultant:

This requires a small investment but I knew the best place to start would be to get objective feedback from a personal image consultant/fashion stylist to get myself headed in the right direction. My personal image consultant helped me enhance my best physical attributes and hide my flaws. One of the first activities we did was to go through various magazines to identify the look that I wanted to achieve. There are so many different looks that a woman can have, such as trendy, classic, eccentric, edgy, understated glam, sexy glam, and chic. I decided I wanted a sexy, casual, chic look and we began planning to achieve it.

The next task was for her to conduct a Closet Inventory. The purpose of the Closet Inventory was to have me try on all the clothes in my closet for two reasons: (1) to see if the clothing help achieve the look that I wanted, and (2) to determine if the fit accented the best aspects of my figure. It literally took about eight hours for me try on all the clothes in my closet. If you cannot afford a personal image consultant at this time, get three of your closest girlfriends to help you conduct a Closet Inventory. Your girlfriends can evaluate how you look in your clothes and vote on which items look great on you versus which items are not very appealing on you. This is fun to do over food, drinks and plenty of laughter. My personal image consultant had also identified my body type, and she knew what type of clothes would look best on my body. As I tried on my clothing, if the item helped to achieve the look and fit my body type, it stayed in the closet. If not, it went into a box of items that were going to be donated to either a family member, friend or the Salvation Army. I had such an emotional tie to certain clothing because I either bought it for a special date or I simply felt cute in it, so I would negotiate to try and keep some pieces in my closet. However, for the most part, if it didn't look good on me nor help me achieve the look I wanted, it was time to part with it. One interesting tip that I learned from the consultant was to establish a relationship with a tailor, as everyone needs a good tailor. Very few of us actually fit in clothes right off the rack. Therefore, a great tailor is needed, because a proper fit can make the quality of the clothes look so much better. Once I had a clear picture of the look that I was trying to achieve and what clothing best fit my body type, I was able to go shopping and buy the clothing that would look best on me and attract the men that I would desire.

Learn to dress for your body type:

My personal image consultant really helped me to hone the art of dressing for my body type. She also recommended a book called *The Science of Sexy* by Bradley Bayou, which helped me better understand this concept. In the book, Bayou, a celebrity stylist, presents a unique style system that caters to every shape and size. His book indicates that the average-size woman is about 5'4", 164 pounds, and size 14, and that real women's bodies are beautiful. The book categorizes your body into one of 48 distinct shapes based upon height, weight and curves, and it offers strategies for dressing sexy depending upon your specific body type. Why buy clothes that don't look great on you? The book helps you dress to balance your body by concealing your flaws and **highlighting** your assets. He teaches that you are judged **by how** you look every time you walk out of the door, regardless of whether you want to be or not. No matter what your size or shape is, this book contains strategies for looking great!

Purchase attractive attire:

Now that I knew what to buy, I was ready to begin shopping with a clear focus and direction. The key items that I added to my wardrobe to achieve my sexy, casual, chic look were fitted jeans, sexy tops, and push-up bras. My favorite designers for sexy tops are Ingwa Melero (more expensive) and the website www.greatglam.com (for very inexpensive sexy tops). Jeans are the Number 1 piece of sexy clothing in my wardrobe. I am very deliberate about the type of jeans that I wear, because a good pair of jeans provides so much flexibility and versatility to my wardrobe. Jeans can be worn with a blazer, sexy top, or tank top. Most important, jeans can make you look thinner, appear to have a larger or smaller butt, or slim down your thighs depending on your goal. All jeans that I purchase are too big in the waist for me. However, knowing the value of a good fitting pair of jeans, I always take them to the tailor to get the best fit. (Check out the website www.zafu.com to find the brand of jeans that best matches your body type.)

Upgrade your hairstyle:

My personal image consultant made a trip with me to my master hairstylist, Barry Fletcher, to get a new look that accented the shape of my face. Some of my goals were to make my hair longer and fuller, which can be accomplished with hair weaves or extensions. I also used the website www.hairstyler.com, which allows you to upload your picture and try on various hairstyles to see how they look on you. I had read a survey that said that the majority of men like long hair, and since I do too, it seemed like an easy choice to create a long, layered, sexy cut.

Receive a face makeover:

I never was big on wearing makeup, but I learned that a little goes a long way. Many of us have never been taught how to effectively apply makeup nor which colors look best on us. So everyone should have a makeup makeover every few years to ensure their look is fresh and modern. The easiest way to get a good makeover is to visit a MAC store (go to www.maccosmetics.com to find a location near you) or a major department store that typically offers free makeovers to help sell their makeup products. I had heard so many good things from friends about MAC that I decided to get my makeover there. I told the MAC consultant about the sexy, casual, chic look that I was going for, and she created a daytime and nighttime look for me. I learned which foundation, shadows and blush color looked best for my complexion. They did a fabulous job and created a look that I can easily maintain on my own. For me, it was important to not have an overly made up look because I wanted something fresh and natural-looking. After the makeover, I realized that I'm still not a big makeup person, but I do love lip gloss. I never wear lipstick, but I have about 20 different lip gloss shades to match various colors. Most days, I only apply a little blush and lip gloss, and for the night time, I step it up with eye makeup. I am still very challenged with the layered eye shadow look; what I do is still not great, but it is acceptable. My makeup routine (foundation, powder, mascara, blush and lip gloss) takes less than five minutes during the day and about 10 minutes at night due to the additional eye makeup to spice it up for the evening. A great book that provides expert secrets for beauty transformations through the use of makeup is called *Makeup Makeovers* by Robert Jones.

Develop a skin care routine:

A skin care routine is critical! There's only so much makeup can do if the skin underneath isn't clear and glowing. Makeup applies and looks so much better on hydrated clear skin. My skin care goal was to have a smooth, even complexion with a healthy glow to make my skin look youthful. I wash my face and moisturize daily with high-end moisturizer by La Mer called Crème de La Mer for very dry skin. I also get a facial about every three to four months for deep cleansing. In between facials, I use a daily face peel by MD Skincare® about twice a week to reveal healthy glowing skin; this product allows my skin to have that healthy glow that I used to have when I was in my early 20s. Proactiv® did a great job clearing my acne, but I also had to use Ambi® for about two months to help clear dark spots left from acne scars. The products that I've mentioned all worked for me, but do your own research and find a skin care routine that works well for your skin. Different products work for different people. The best objective site that I've found to help get reviews from real women on various cosmetic products is www.makeupalley.com. Additionally, one of the first books that opened my eyes to beauty and skin care was by Tyra Banks called *Tyra's Beauty Inside and Out*. Even though it's been years since I've read it, I remember learning so many great tips and strategies, most of which I still use today.

Reshape your eyebrows:

The shape of your eyebrows will help define your entire face. For me, the one thing that I am extremely particular about is my eyebrows. My eyebrows naturally grow full, so I have to shape them to properly fit my facial features. One time, a lady waxed my brows in a pencil thin shape that was arched really high. I was devastated and it looked horrible. It took months for them to grow back in properly. So now, after I consulted with a new esthetician, I have her maintain my eyebrows every two weeks. I've seen women just come into a nail salon, sit in the chair, and let the technician wax their eyebrows without any discussion about the look they're trying to achieve. That is not a good approach. Instead, take a look at any style or beauty magazine, and you'll notice that eyebrows come in many different shapes. Pick an eyebrow shape that matches your facial features. A good brow shaping can enhance your face shape and contours.

Leverage hair, skin and nail vitamins:

I also used vitamins to improve my hair and skin. These were specialty vitamins targeted to help your hair, skin and nails look healthier and grow faster. I normally take multivitamins daily, but certain vitamins like Niacin and Biotin are key vitamins that help the skin and hair specifically.

Maintaining Optimal Health

Over the years, I've learn to apply the same rigor I applied to achieving outer physical beauty to building optimal inner health. Both are important. To achieve optimal health, I've used the following techniques to reduce aging, ensure a strong immune system, and maintain energy, health and vitality. I included these techniques because how you look and feel are a key success factor for attracting more men into your life. The four most notable techniques that I used to achieve optimal health are:

✤ Colonics/colon cleansing:

If I didn't believe so strongly in proper colon health, I would really have skipped this topic in the book. However, one of the best ways that I've maintained optimal health over the years is through maintaining proper colon health. For about the last 10 years, I've done a colon cleansing to detoxify my body and cleanse my bowel and eliminate the toxins that have built up in my digestive system. My favorite product has been by Dr. Natura (www.drnatura.com). One year, I even got a colonic, which is when a colon therapist injects an infusion of water into the rectum to cleanse and flush out the colon. The purpose of the colonic was to remove accumulated waste and toxins from the colon, to help prevent constipation, and improve overall health. The colonic was helpful, but the process was uncomfortable, not painful, but just kind of weird. Since then, I only do the annual colon cleansers and have been really pleased with the results.

✤ Oxygen therapies:

I first learned about oxygen therapies at a natural health food store. I was looking for some type of vitamin to boost my immune system since I kept getting colds frequently. I've used oxygen therapies for about 10 years now, and in that timeframe, I have been sick only about two times, compared to being sick about every two to three months. I used to always be under the weather, or recovering from a cold or flu, or just getting a cold. Oxygen therapies alter the body's chemistry to help overcome disease, promote repair, and improve overall function. Oxygen therapy is an alternative medical treatment that has been used to treat a wide variety of conditions, including infections (viral, fungal, parasitic, bacterial), circulatory problems, chronic fatigue syndrome, arthritis, allergies and cancer. I have used intravenous oxygen injections as well as stabilized liquid oxygen and have gotten great results. Some athletes sleep in hyperbaric oxygen chambers to expedite healing from injuries. I've spent many hours studying articles and books on oxygen therapies, and you should do the same to determine if it can be helpful to you. A book I would recommend on the topic is called *Flood Your Body with Oxygen* by Ed McCabe.

✺ Green Tea:

I began drinking green tea after a co-worker recommended it to me to increase my energy levels. After doing research I found that the right green tea can have amazing benefits, which I have experienced. I drink a cup of Okuma's Wu-Long tea (www.wulongforlife.com) daily and it has helped to boost my energy levels, clear my skin, and assist in reducing body fat, in conjunction with proper exercise and diet. There have been many scientific studies about the benefits of green tea, but I would recommend it based upon my personal experience in using it. I really understand why it is nicknamed the "slimming tea."

✦ **Acupuncture:**

I used acupuncture a few times to help minimize PMS symptoms and cramping. I thought acupuncture was helpful and very relaxing. I didn't continue acupuncture after the first year because seeing those little needles all over me was just plain scary. I felt like I was a character in a horror film.

The Results of My Beauty Transformation

As a result of maintaining my beauty regimen, I have been able to get my fair share of dates over the years. In fact, dating has become more fun each year. I think my beauty transformation has been one of the most effective things that I have done to increase the quantity of dates that I am able to get. I can personally attest to the fact that men are very visual creatures and a woman's physical appearance is what gets their attention. I even had men that I knew in high school asking me out after my beauty transformation!

CHAPTER FOUR

Strippin' Ain't Easy

So I Think I Can Dance

To me, one of the most fun things to do is to go dancing. Ever since I was a young child, I loved to dance. When I was about four or five years old, my parents would have house parties. I would sneak out of the bedroom and go participate in all the fun. I would get my dance on as much as possible because as soon as my mother caught me, she would make me go back to bed. But not before my aunts would teach me some new moves, which I'd work on and practice until the next house party.

My love of dancing led me to become a DJ (aka DJ Roma) about five years ago. Whenever I was at a party, I would complain about how bad the DJ was and would want to make recommendations to him that would really bring the party alive. One of my friends said, "If you know so much about DJing, then why don't you do it?" I thought to myself, This is a good idea, because I know music, dancing and how to have a good time at a party. Over time, friends and family would ask me to play music at summer BBQs and that springboarded my DJ career, which now consists of weddings, corporate events, and birthday parties. I take a lot of pride in my love for dancing, music and DJing and look at my dancing abilities as one of my strengths.

I was always confident that I was a great dancer until I met a guy I called the "Strip Club Genius." I called him that because one of his favorite pastimes was going to strip clubs with his friends. The guy knew a lot about how good strippers dance. One day, while I was cooking us dinner, I was showing off my great dancing abilities. This is nothing new for me as I dance while getting dressed for work, cleaning the house and, sometimes, for no reason at all. As I proceeded to dance as I cooked dinner, the Strip Club Genius told me that "you can't dance at all and really needed to learn how!" I looked at him and said, "What?!" He replied, "I'm not trying to hurt your feelings, but it's true... you really can't dance." Imagine how much of a shock this was to me. I was totally floored. He said, "If you're going to dance for me, you need to make your booty clap and drop it like it's hot." I told him, "First of all, I am not dancing *for you*." I went on to explain that I was a DJ and a great dancer. Since the Genius realized that he had offended me, I think he thought he should guide me in the right direction. He then said, "I'm going to show you the type of dancing you need to do for a man." He took his laptop and searched online for Nelly's "Tip Drill" video. When he played this music video, I saw that it showed a household full of women doing dances like I'd never seen before. I said that this kind of dancing takes "dirty dancing" to a whole new level. He seemed surprised that I was unfamiliar with these dances. He remarked, "This is how all the women in the strip club dance; and this is how you need to dance for a man." I politely told him thanks for sharing, and continued to do my tired little dances throughout the night.

Over the next few days, I thought, I refuse to have him or anyone else tell me that I cannot dance! I think the Strip Club Genius knew that I was bothered by his comments and he sent me a text message later in the week that said, "I'm sorry that I said you couldn't dance, but it's true." As if this text made me feel any better.

So I Learn to Striptease

My competitive nature wouldn't let me settle with being called a bad dancer. The next week, when I was walking past a gym, I saw a flyer for a Striptease 101 class and stopped into the dance studio to inquire more about it. After the instructor told me more about the class, I immediately enrolled. It was a class for sexy, erotic dancing, which was new to me, but it sure sounded like fun. I had a simple goal, to learn to dance like those women in the "Tip Drill" video. Hey, I consider myself a simple-minded woman; whoever said your goals in life had to be grand or lofty?

For the first class, they had encouraged us to wear tight-fitting shorts and a top, along with platform heels, and to bring water. I was very committed to my new goal, so I had to go purchase some platforms heels. I even thought about buying some clear heels, but I thought that would be taking it too far, and plus, I couldn't find any at the major department stores where I shopped. I remember the first class was on a Sunday, and as I was packing my bag for striptease class, I thought, My butt should be going to church instead! But this was the only day the class was offered and I wasn't going to miss this class for anything in the world.

I packed my bag and headed to class. As I arrived there, I was pleased to find that the instructor was a heavy, voluptuous Black woman who was about 40 years old. I thought that if she could striptease, than so could I. I originally had concerns about not being young enough to striptease because none of the girls in the video looked to be a day over 25.

The first assignment in the class was to give ourselves a name that represented our sexy stripper persona. My name was Bootylicious, which just felt right for me. We begin the class with a few sexy walks, looks and other flirtatious techniques. This is when I first realized that I had no clue about how to flirt and be sexy. Growing up as a tomboy, I knew a lot about men, but not always how to attract them. So I was already beginning to get benefits from the class beyond my expectations. We later moved into a sexy striptease routine where we learned numerous great sexy dance moves.

I had no idea of how fun, yet difficult this class would be. The next day when I woke up, I could barely move my arms, hips and thighs; I was so sore that I could barely get out the bed without grimacing. I never had a workout in my life where I felt that much pain. After a few days when the pain had subsided, I was excited about going to the next class. I knew I was onto something good. I continued taking striptease classes every week and had found a fun new hobby.

After I told one of my guy friends about my new striptease classes, he suggested that I go to a real strip club with him so I can see my skills compared to the working ladies. My first response was "Hell no!" and then I thought since I'd never been to a strip club, it might be fun. Later that week, my friends and I were off to the strip clubs in the dark alleys of Baltimore. There were about eight of us, half of us women, half of the group men, and I found out that I was the only one who had never been to a strip club. All of the women took pride in having visited strip clubs in the past with their boyfriends to add fun and excitement to their relationships. I thought, I really need to get out of the house more!

The first club we went to was a hip-hop strip club with various Black women of all shapes and sizes. Two things that I noticed while I was there; one, that many of the strippers were thick, but tone. And two, they all knew how to dance on the pole.

We later went to another strip club that was full of White women and too much red velvet. In this place I noticed two things; one, all the White strippers were skinny with big breasts, and two, they all knew how to work the pole.

I then decided that a pole dance routine was missing from my current striptease classes. I decided to search for some local pole dance classes as the next step in my journey. Once I found the pole dance "'exercise" class, I immediately enrolled and anxiously awaited the next adventure. Let me first say that the women who work the pole for a living are extremely talented and acrobatic. I quickly learned how talented they must be to lift and swing their bodies from the pole with such ease and grace. I now know for sure that "strippin' ain't easy." After my first pole dance class, I had several bruises and nicks from banging into the pole. However, I noticed that my arms received an incredible workout due to having to lift my entire body by my arms. Given that my arms have never been tight or tone, this was an added benefit that the pole dance class provided.

There were about five advanced levels for the pole dance class, and each required completion of a six-week class. As you might guess, I was determined to complete all of the advanced levels so that I could be a great pole dancer. To help myself achieve this goal, I purchased a retractable pole so that I could practice at home. This pole was very inexpensive, only a few hundred dollars, and its retractable nature allowed me to take it down so that my guests wouldn't think I lived some type of secret life. To say that I was serious about my pole dance class is an understatement. I went and bought new outfits and practiced regularly so that I could advance to the next level. My goal was to complete all the advanced levels so that I could be a great pole dancer, and I was very pleased with my progress.

As a result of my striptease and pole dance classes, I begin to receive the best workout of my life, including both upper and lower body toning. I was soon in the best physical condition of my life. I even took a few sexy chair-routine lap dance classes as well. I ended up also losing about 10 pounds, and I developed tight, toned muscles in my arms and legs. These classes had exceeded all of my expectations.

My striptease and pole dance classes helped me to embrace my sexuality. I now think of myself as sexy regardless of whether or not I'm about to have sex. I dress and walk in a way that makes me feel sexy and confident. As women, we have to be comfortable with our sexuality in order to please a man and meet his needs. Men are drawn to women who are comfortable with their sexual identity. So maintain a healthy view of sex and be open to new experiences that help you embrace your sexuality.

The guy who started me on my striptease/pole dance journey never got to see the results, but I appreciate him for starting me on this path. Growing up with many brothers, I've always been really competitive. If someone says I can't do something, that's an automatic reason for me to prove to them that I can. I know my striptease and pole dance classes were not taken for a man, but for my own personal empowerment and physical fitness. To this day, no man has ever benefited from my new striptease/pole dance skills, but I take so much pride in what I have learned. And the fitness results I get from the classes have caused me to stick with striptease/pole dance as my fitness routine of choice. It's just simply fun and sexy.

CHAPTER FIVE

I'm His Wife, Not His Girlfriend

I believe that true love and passion are real and authentic, but many times, marriage is not. I feel that too many married couples are pretending to be happy. I personally know many couples who are not truly happy in a fully committed monogamous marriage. The fact is that the old model of marriage is clearly not working as evidenced by the divorce statistics, which indicate that over half of marriages end in divorce. Some researchers say that at least 75% of marriages are ailing or unhappy. For African Americans, divorce is the end result for two out of three Black marriages. When I found out this information, it was startling to me, and over the last few years, I have been studying about marriage and divorce to understand why these challenges exist today. It's not that I don't believe in marriage. In fact, I do believe in the institution of marriage. My parents shared a great marriage for over 20 years by the time my dad passed away. I grew up in a household where the marriage relationship was happy and healthy. It was just important for me to understand how to make my own marriage work.

Most marriages, on the surface, seem like a typical traditional marriage, but many of them are truly unhappy. This leads me to believe that marriage may be in a process of transitioning from our "parent's generation" marriage to a type of more contemporary or modern marriage that will work for people today. However, many us do not know how to achieve this type of marriage, or know what this type of marriage looks like.

Many will agree that marriage can be convenient, however, with too much routine and definition, marriage can be the death of a love relationship. Too many people have squeezed the love affair out of their marriage and have allowed bills, money, and/or petty arguments to block the romantic aspects of their relationship. While I was married, I wanted to be free to grow, develop and experience new things and people. When I was unmarried, I wanted the security and stability that a marriage relationship provides. Unmarried women feel sorry for married women because they tend to be stuck in a rut or routine. Married women feel sorry for unmarried woman because they are alone. However, we all want both excitement and stability in our relationships whether we're married or unmarried.

Current State of Marriage/Why Do People Get Married?

People often marry because it's the tradition. Men and women have been getting married since before recorded history. Until recently, America was the most "married" nation in the world. But now many ask, "Do I have to be married to live happily ever after?" In today's society, people have a strong desire to simply be happy, whether that means being married or unmarried. Today fewer get married and more get divorced, and the unmarried and divorced population is growing. The cost of divorce can be both financially and emotionally devastating, and many are avoiding marriage just to ensure that they never have to go through divorce. With many marriages ailing or failing, some couples are considering various marriage alternatives in order to make informed intelligent decisions about their own lives.

Romantic love has been the primary motive for getting married, and it remains so even today. However, there are other factors that cause individuals to marry. Years ago there were more traditional reasons for getting married. Women wanted to get out of their parents' homes, lose their virginity, or gain financial stability. In turn, men wanted a wife to care for them or help them fulfill their role as a husband and provider. Both men and women wanted to have children and raise a family. Marriage was definitely created to raise children. Back in the day, couples stayed together because they had to remain married. The wife was a homemaker and didn't have a lot of options. Husbands were the family's only provider so he would be perceived horribly if he left. However, today many of these motives for getting married no longer apply. Most men don't really expect a woman to devote her entire life to him and his upkeep, and likewise, many women no longer rely on men to pay their way. Additionally, we rarely find women who want to marry just to have sex. Even pregnancy doesn't lead a couple to marry as it had in the past. Marriage in America has truly changed due to social and cultural influences. For better or for worse, this is the current state of marriage.

As much as I was concerned about my own marriage, I couldn't help thinking about the current state of marriage overall and how the changes in marriage affect society today and in the future. I think that people want to really make sense of their own lives, and to understand how societal and cultural forces have shaped marriage today. I, myself, wanted to better understand the new contemporary marriage models and the marrying trends of our current generation.

Making My Marriage Work

Around the time I decided to research why marriage was struggling, I was having trouble understanding why my marriage to the man I loved and married before God and all of our family and friends was simply not working. I wondered if I had made a huge mistake and if I should have never gotten married in the first place. This was very sad for me because I truly married the man of my dreams who I loved so much, but we were having difficulty in our marriage.

From the first day I met my husband, it was as if we were born friends. Even today, my ex-husband is still my best friend who I love dearly. As we grew closer initially as a couple, I considered myself to be practical, loyal, organized, emotionally strong, and responsible. Plus, my husband met all of the characteristics and traits that I wanted in a husband. He is a great guy, a person of integrity, very successful in his career, with a similar Southern background as I had. We were an attractive couple, well educated, successful in business, with active social lives and hobbies. From the outside looking in, we looked like the "power couple" who appeared to be perfect for each other.

I never believed much in the concept of a soulmate until

I met my husband. I felt that we were deeply connected from the first day we met. We were spiritually and professionally compatible, with a great amount of chemistry and attraction to each other. This is what led me to believe that we might actually be soulmates. However we were naive in thinking early on that what we had was enough to make marriage work. Over the years, we learned that we were not emotionally or physically compatible and did not have the same expectations. We could have easily called it quits because we had no kids together and were both financially stable; yet, we knew there were some valuable aspects of our relationship that were worth salvaging. This is why we decided to seek alternative marriage options that would work for us.

Looking back on my marriage, I would describe the love from my husband as a suffocating love. Sometimes I thought he loved me too much. He always wanted to be near me, for me to listen to his concerns, and to advise him about his work relationships, business and hobbies. He thought I was good for him, and I have to admit, I thought he was good for me. Originally, it felt great to get all that attention, but eventually, the level of intimacy that he required was more than I could give. Trying to be his wife and girlfriend was too much work for me. Between maintaining our home, doing laundry, working every day, dating him every evening, and talking to him every day, our marriage was a huge responsibility for me. On my side of things, I require very little emotional and physical interaction on a day-to-day basis. However, my husband had an incredibly high need for emotional and physical connection, including physical intimacy, as well as intimate communications. I remember telling him, "You need to go get a girlfriend or something because I can't be your wife and your girlfriend!" Within our marriage, I had difficulty finding enough time for me and for him; if I met all of his needs, there was no time left for me to be me.

I know for me and others I know, marriage can feel restrictive and sometimes isolating. I believe it is a high expectation to have our spouse meet all of our physical, emotional and spiritual needs. For me, if my husband acknowledged that he was attracted to someone else, that made perfect sense. It actually seemed normal and reasonable. I didn't think that he would never be attracted to anyone else because he was married to me.

For one of my close friends, about five years of exclusive commitment was the longest time that she could be monogamous with any one person. She would often grow bored, restless and desire something new and different. She would usually leave that relationship and seek a new partner, only to find, after four to five years, that same restless feeling. However, alternative open relationships were never discussed or considered. I've known many men and women who have loved more than one person over many years, but pursuing other relationships just wasn't generally accepted or discussed.

Because my husband and I loved each other, it was important for us to forget about what being married was supposed to look like and create a marriage that would work for us. We began our journey to figure out how to make the marriage work for us. I have been excited about what I've learned regarding the ways to redefine a relationship so it can be more open, intimate, loving and authentic. For I believe so strongly that love is gift to us, and it runs deep and sustains us in the midst of a chaotic world. We desperately wanted our marriage relationship to work for us.

As a result of my studies, I learned that my husband and I were positioned for an "open marriage," which had less to do about sex with other people, but more to do about strengthening our own partnership and commitment to one another. We chose to hold on to some material, emotional and spiritual aspects of our marriage, while letting go of the monogamous agreement that typically comes with a traditional marriage. We refused to have a marriage where we dragged ourselves to bed and had no intellectual, emotional or spiritual connection. To us, that marriage is not authentic and does not serve its purpose.

Likewise, it was important for me and my husband to forget about what marriage is supposed to look like and to create a marriage that would work for us. Even though my personality didn't allow me to be overly concerned about what friends or co-workers thought, we did care deeply about what our family thought. For family has always been extremely important to me and I cared about what they thought or how this would impact them.

We decided to let God guide our hearts to explore options that would help to maintain our commitment to one other. To us, commitment doesn't mean you have to be sexually exclusive to each other. It was important for us to redefine our relationship based upon our needs and values.

I encourage you to create your own vision of an ideal relationship, also based upon your needs and values.

Identify your true desires in life by asking yourself what you want from your relationship. As an example, do you prefer to live alone and have several outside, meaningful relationships where you spend quality time with different partners? Instead of cheating or unfaithfulness, practice being faithful and honest to all your friends/lovers about your needs and desires. This allows you to be open and honest and honor your commitment to one another. My husband and I maintained an open marriage for two years and still remain best friends today.

An ironic part of our story is something that happened one day when I was preparing for a trial date for a traffic ticket I had received a few months earlier. I was searching for documentation that I needed to take to court with me. During the search, I found our signed marriage license certificates in the bottom of one of the piles and thought that this information should have probably been turned into the courthouse. After I won my traffic court case, I went to check the government database for our records and there was no sign of our marriage license. Agents searched several computers to try and find our marriage record and concluded that we were not legally married because no one had ever turned in our signed marriage license certificates. This development is the reason I call him my ex-husband, but still today he is my best friend in life. Because we were technically never married, we never had to make the decision to divorce. We have a beautiful relationship today and remain very committed to each other's development and success in life. We spend quality time together, especially holidays and family functions, and I couldn't see my life without him in it.

PART II
THE DATING
ACTION PLAN:

*Become the Woman
that Every Man Wants*

THE DATING ACTION PLAN:

Become the Woman that Every Man Wants

Many women work hard to find a good man, but don't spend enough time making sure that they are the "right woman" that he is looking for. Be sure that you become all that a man will desire so that he'll feel like you are his top choice.

In this section, you'll learn the specific strategies that will help you become an exciting and highly desirable woman. These strategies have been successfully applied by other women who have achieved great success in their love life. Use these strategies in your daily life, and you will begin to see dating as fun and enjoyable. This approach will also lead you to the love you desire.

Be open to new experiences and expect to fail a few times as you began to take control of your dating life. Expect some rejections, but let the sting of rejection roll off your back. Keep pressing forward! Never give up on seeking the love you deserve.

CHAPTER SIX

Unpack Your Baggage

I was speaking to a male friend of mine about why he and his girlfriend broke up, and he emphatically said, "She got issues." He didn't have to explain further; I knew this meant that her emotional baggage was so great that it manifested in her behavior, attitudes and conversation. Don't bring emotional baggage into a new relationship! It is our responsibility to get rid of our emotional baggage, which is that buildup of negative emotional energy from hurts and wounds from our past. If you have a lot of emotional baggage, please get help before you worry about dating and getting involved in a new relationship.

Everyone can think of some circumstance or situation in their past that might prevent them from achieving their dreams. Some use the challenges and disappointments from their past to motivate themselves to move in a new direction or change their circumstances. They use painful past experiences to inspire themselves to greater heights and deeper depths in life. But others live in the past every day. The only way your past will become your present is if you choose to live in the past. The reason it's called the past is because that's all behind us.

Some of us have some deep hurts and wounds from our childhood that have not been dealt with. Those hurts and wounds that occur within the first seven years of life play the most significant role in your development. They often leave deep psychological wounds that rob us of becoming our best self. As a result, we walk through life wounded, not allowing our best gifts, abilities and talents to shine. Issues of abandonment, abuse or neglect have to be dealt with or they will manifest themselves in our adult relationships and impede our ability to establish meaningful love relationships. By healing, you prepare yourself for a healthy love and begin to attract healthier partners. Instead of two wounded people coming together, you'll attract healthy, whole partners into your life. When you try to date as a wounded person, you look for your partner to make you whole or to help you feel better. It is unfair to look for someone else to heal us. It is not their responsibility to fix us, it is ours.

Please do not go through life thinking of yourself as a victim. Don't hold on to all the wrongs that were done to you as a child. Some of you were brought up in dysfunctional families, and you may have had to deal with rape, incest or other forms of violence. Even so, there comes a time in your life where you have to take control and move beyond those injustices. If you have persistent emotional distress or reminders of painful past events in your life, time spent with a psychologist to get emotional help or a better mental perspective may be valuable for you.

Think about a relationship in your past that ended very badly. Can you remember why it was bad? Was it due to you and your issues, his issues, or just bad timing? Now think of other relationships in your past, and see if you can identify any pattern of relationship failures. Were you always jealous, rude or nasty? Was he always unavailable or involved with someone else? I've often heard that we will repeat the same mistakes in life until we learn from them. So it is important to gain the lesson and avoid the same mistakes in future relationships. Go forward, and identify your mistakes in life as "learning experiences." There really are no true mistakes in life, but only opportunities to learn and grow. Similar learning opportunities will continue until you get the point of the lesson.

For any past bad relationships, remember what you learned, and apply the lesson to future relationships. However, leave the hurt and disappointment in the past. Too many times we sum up new people based on prior experiences with those who were similar to them. When you first meet a man, be sure to judge him for who he is based on his own merits, not based on any preconceived notions.

One way to learn from your past experiences is to notice the warning signs associated with painful relationships in the past. When those warning signs appear, steer clear of making the same mistakes again. It becomes personally frustrating when we repeat the same mistakes in life. That means we are not growing and developing spiritually or emotionally.

When I was younger and more immature about how I dated, I didn't know that the end of the relationship was a likely outcome. I was always trying to avoid the relationship from ending. Then when the guy and I inevitably stopped seeing each other, I'd dwell on that loss day and night. I'd think about the relationship for months, and I held on to the gifts and cards—even special emails or photos. I've learned by now that I don't need to hold onto any reminders of bad relationships. In fact, I don't need any reminders or emotional attachments to anything painful in my past. It slows down the healing process by dwelling on earlier times. Nowadays if I stop dating a guy, I rarely keep the number in my cell phone, much less any cards or gifts. Don't penalize your future love life by holding on to destructive and painful memories from your past. Also, if your relationship failure was due to a bad lapse in judgment, a once-in-a-lifetime mistake, forgive yourself and move on to your next relationship opportunity.

Action Item:

Think of your past failed relationships. Next, write down why each relationship ended and what you learned from the relationships. Be sure to learn from these mistakes and avoid them in future relationships.

CHAPTER SEVEN

Love Yourself First

I believe love is a gift and love always begins with us. You must love yourself in order to love others. Love is a process of giving and receiving. You won't know how to give away love unless you possess it within yourself first. Likewise, you can't receive love if you don't feel that you truly deserve it. However, we all deserve healthy, satisfying love relationships.

In order to attract love into your life, it's important to improve the relationship you have with yourself. If you love yourself and have confidence in who you are, you'll begin to send a signal to others that you have value and deserve respect. An improved sense of self will lead you to a more fulfilling love life. Loving yourself first sends a clear message that you are to be recognized, celebrated, appreciated and loved.

Sometimes our sense of self-worth or self-esteem is shaped by the people in our inner circle. Some of us have family members and friends ruining our self-esteem every day. Even if they are your flesh and blood, try to remove yourself from their presence as much as possible. Hurtful words negate any progress towards self-worth and self-love.

Just by virtue of being born, you are loved. As long as we are alive and breathing, we are never separate from God's love. In these ways, love always exists in our life. Do believe that God created you exactly the way He wanted and equipped you with everything you need to live a fulfilling abundant life. Believe that God has given you everything you need to fulfill your heart's desire. You have to be confident that you have the gifts, talents, looks and strengths to fulfill your destiny in life.

It is also important to love your physical appearance and what you look like. It is important to get comfortable with your body. You must appreciate and accept who you are on a physical level. Elsewhere in the book, I discuss how to maximize your physical beauty, but here I will simply say love your body. Loving your body is about having a healthy body, regardless of your size or body type. And you do this through a healthy diet, exercise and sleep/relaxation. A healthy body is a sexy body. Luckily, men love the many colors, shapes and sizes that we come in, and we appreciate men for letting us know how beautiful we are as women.

If you don't truly know yourself and what you want out of a relationship, how can you attract the right man into your life? Before you can truly know what you want out of a relationship, you have to have a sense of what your needs and wants are and what truly makes you happy.

One important step in loving yourself is when you stop trying to please everybody else in your life. As we grew up, we often would try to make our mom or dad proud, our teachers, and maybe our pastors, but as an adult, we don't have the time or energy to try and constantly please others. You will have to prioritize your own needs over the needs of others. I know this may sound selfish; however, once you adjust to this concept, you'll free up more time and energy for yourself.

I have always been pretty good about attending to my needs and putting myself first. Growing up, I always had to stand up for myself in a house full of boys. If one of them teased me, my mom would say, "Go back and stand up for yourself." And so I would.

When I was younger, I dated a man who always put his needs before mine. He needed a favor, or some money to hold him over, or a ride somewhere. I've learned that there is nothing wrong with making sacrifices for some-one else, but not if it always comes at my expense. On occasion, a favor is fine, but if the man is not making adjustments or sacrifices for you, then stand up for your-self. You shouldn't be the only one inconvenienced in the relationship. You will need to maintain a sense of control in your romantic relationship, so speak up for what you want and need in life.

As women, we are mothers, wives, daughters, sisters, employees, business owners, and sometimes we perform all of these roles within the same hour of the day. Women have experienced a lot and continue to be the rock of the family. We all have those moments when we endure life's tests and others where we overcome great challenges. Therefore, it is important to remember your personal breakthroughs in life and draw strength from them. These triumphant times increase our self-esteem.

When I was in my early 20s, I had a fear of public speak-ing. Those who know me now find this very hard to believe as I tend to be rather communicative most of the time. But when I worked for a large management consult-ing firm, a partner once told me, "You have great ideas. However, if you don't learn to communicate them in front of people, it's like you have no ideas at all." (I write about this in Chapter 2.) But I knew the reality was that getting in front of a group and speaking scared me to death. I decided to address my fear of public speaking by enrolling in the Dale Carnegie Course, which is designed to help you overcome your fear of public speaking and improve your interpersonal skills. After successfully completing the training program, I knew I was ready to put my new skills to the test. At a company meeting, I was asked to give a presentation on IT Strategic Planning and normally I would have found a way to get out of that assignment. However, this time I was ready. After I gave my presentation, which was only about 10 minutes long, I felt on top of the world. I thought to myself, I did it and I didn't pass out. That was a great feeling!

Laugh at Yourself

In addition to loving yourself, you must learn to laugh at yourself. I think everyone would agree that having a great sense of humor is a positive trait. By laughing at yourself and not taking yourself too seriously, it really takes the pressure and edge off everyday life.

I remember when I was in college, I interned at an IT company in the summers. Every year we had an annual cookout, with plenty of food and games. I always enjoyed playing volleyball, which was one of my favorite sports growing up. Well, my second summer with the company, I decided to sign up for volleyball as I did the previous year. However, this summer, I was wearing wigs to enhance my look. Looking back at the photos, I'm not so sure that particular wig really improved my look. Nonetheless, I got dressed for volleyball and went out to play. As I begin to jump up and down, it never occurred to me that my wig was starting to loosen a bit. Then I went to spike the ball, and I went forward and my wig went backwards. It was like a slow motion segment in a movie; I watched the wig falling to the ground, but I couldn't do anything to stop it. As the wig lay entangled in the sand on the ground, I didn't know whether to pick it up or run to my car. Everyone stood there looking at me and my head, which was covered in a wig cap. After a quiet moment, I burst into laughter, because I thought this was the funniest thing that had happened to me in years. In a matter of seconds, everyone else was violently laughing; they were keeling over, some even on the knees giggling, and having a blast. I was genuinely tickled by this whole turn of events and had so much fun laughing and making the most of a very bad situation. The next day, and subsequent days, we continued to laugh at this incident. From that day forward, all of the instances in my life that would naturally be embarrassing for some have become the funniest moments in my life.

Make a Commitment to You

Commit to developing a relationship with yourself. Learn to say no to others so you can spend more time learning and meeting your needs. Commit time to doing things that you enjoy that are just for you. Some of us are so busy at work, church, and family obligations that we neglect time with ourselves. But you need to carve out time to invest in you. Some things you could do for yourself include:

～ Sign up for a new class related to a hobby.

～ Learn to play your favorite musical instrument.

～ Paint and redecorate a room in your house.

～ Learn to cook a new meal or dessert that you like.

～ Do some volunteer work.

～ Watch your favorite movie.

～ Learn a new sport.

～ Schedule a photo shoot and become a model for a day.

～ Do some gardening.

～ Learn a new foreign language.

～ Curl up in bed on a Saturday morning and read a good book.

～ Make a massage or facial appointment at a nice spa.

～ Watch a comedy movie and laugh out loud.

～ Enjoy a glass of wine and relax all evening.

Action Item:

Create a list of activities that you are going to do just for you; those activities that bring you enjoyment in life. Once you identify these activities, schedule them on your calendar to ensure that they don't get overlooked due to other priorities. Make yourself a priority in your life.

CHAPTER EIGHT

Determine Your Relationship Market Value (RMV)

Before you begin the dating process, it's important to understand your Relationship Market Value (RMV). Your RMV helps you determine three things: (1) the characteristics that you bring to a relationship that can be of value or benefit to a mate; (2) what type of guys you can attract so that you can focus your efforts on finding that type of man; and (3) if you are ready for a relationship. When determining your Relationship Market Value, you take a close look at your mental/emotional health, financial health, family relationships and other areas of your life, and discover if you are *really* ready for a relationship.

You determine your RMV by looking at the positive traits that you bring to the table that add value to the relationship, while evaluating the negative ones as well—those that may take something away or create challenges in a relationship. Determining your value is about being realistic regarding what you will be bringing into a relationship. Sometimes people are frustrated in relationships because they are always dating people who are not in their lane or out of their league. If you are constantly frustrated or getting rejected, evaluate your RMV and be honest with yourself. Don't always try to be a romantic overachiever and then ask why you can never find a man. If you have some

RMV Assessment Area	Description	Ranking
Physical Appearance/ Your Looks	Although beauty is in the eye of the beholder, most would agree that some people are naturally prettier than others. Please assess how attractive or pretty you are (as others see you). Factor in both your facial features and body/figure. Assume a 10 would be someone like Halle Berry and a 1 would be someone like "Ugly Betty."	
Career or Job Stability	Do you have a career with a solid income or are you still working at McDonalds at 30 years old? We know that all work is respectable; however, the degree of your success in your career or job determines the type of mate you attract.	
Spiritual/ Emotional/ Mental Stability	Are you an emotionally stable person? Do you have strong values and beliefs that guide your day-to-day life? Are you insecure, jealous or angry? Do you believe in a Higher Power greater than you?	

RMV Assessment Area	Description	Ranking
Financial Stability	Are you financially stable with savings, investments and good credit? Also, take a look at your take-home pay vs. your bills and debt to determine your current financial situation.	
Personality/ Interpersonal Skills	Do you have interesting things in life to share or talk about? Do you have many friends? Are people interested in spending time with you? Are you fun to be around? Do people enjoy being around you?	
Family Relationships	Do you have strong family ties or are all of your current family relationships dysfunctional? Do you have any children; if so, how many and how well-behaved and disciplined are your children?	

RMV Assessment Area	Description	Ranking
Education/ Training	Do you have a college degree or an advanced degree, or did you not attend college at all? Is your college degree from an Ivy League school or an adult night college? Be sure to consider the quality of your college education as well.	
Social or Celebrity Status	Are you well connected with "high society" folks? Have you been to the elite country clubs across the country? Do you have access to celebrity events or parties that are hard to get tickets for?	
Homemaker Skills	Do you keep a clean house? How does your home look on most days? Can you cook really well? Would you be good at raising children?	

real negative traits, such as being broke or having eight children, those things are not going to be perceived positively by a lot of men. One of my negative traits, gambling, probably rules out the possibility of me marrying a pastor. (But I enjoy gambling.) It is important to know your strengths and build upon them so that you can differentiate yourself from other women. If you are funny, be the funniest, wittiest woman in the room. If you are pretty, smile and be proud to be the most attractive woman in the room.

Personal Discovery and Self-Assessment

Before you can determine your RMV, it's important to do some personal discovery and self-assessment. You must know what your God-given talents, strengths and abilities are, and use them to create a life that you enjoy. This is important because a man is supposed to enhance your life, not save you from your own life. To begin the discovery and assessment process, ask yourself the following questions:

* What are you passionate about?

* What are your beliefs and values in life?

* Are you spiritual or are you religious, and do you know the difference?

* Do you want kids or do you even like kids, especially other people's kids?

* Are you a hot-head or impatient with people, or are you easy-going and laidback?

* Do you need a lot of physical and emotional intimacy?

* What do you do for fun or entertainment?

* Are you educated or street smart, or have you not read a book or newspaper in over a year (magazines don't count!)?

* Are you social or outgoing, or do you enjoy alone time at home?

* What do you want to achieve in life? What are your career goals?

* Are you prone to spend money or save money?

* What are your personal breakthroughs?

* What are your major accomplishments in life?

Action Item:

Answer each question above so you can maintain a clear picture in your mind of who you are and the characteristics that are important to you.

Determining Your RMV

Now that you've completed the personal discovery and self-assessment questions, let's determine your Relationship Market Value. Give yourself a rating (on a scale of 1 to 10, 10 being the highest ranking) for all the areas noted below. For the areas where you scored a 7 or higher, consider those to be the strengths or positive traits that you bring to a relationship. For areas that are 3 or lower, those would be considered traits that would likely be perceived negatively by men. You'll want to use your positive traits to help attract the type of man who would value the best in you. Since we sometimes have a hard time seeing ourselves the way others see us, you may want to ask a close friend to complete the RMV assessment for you.

Now that you have completed your RMV assessment, how should you use it? Well, first it's important to realize that we tend to attract people into our life who are similar to us. If you have a college degree, which is a positive trait, then you can likely attract a man who is college educated also. To contrast, if you have five children, by two different men, you will not likely attract a man who has no children. To him, the fact that you have five children would likely be perceived as a negative trait. Use your RMV to determine what type of guys you can attract, then you can begin to focus your efforts on finding that type of man. This will not just be any man, but the right man *for you*.

Action Item:

Determine your Relationship Market Value
and use that to guide yourself toward the type of
men who will value your positive traits.

CHAPTER NINE

Fix Your Fatal Flaws

Have you ever met a guy you really liked and thought you hit it off well, but he never called you again? And not only did he never call again, he wouldn't even return your calls anymore, so you have no idea as to why he stopped calling? It could have either been because he's involved with someone else, or you did something to turn him off. But what's most annoying is that you really don't know why he never contacted you again. Well, oftentimes we have some weakness or fatal flaw that really spooked the guy or turned him off. That's why it is your responsibility to identify and fix your fatal flaws (weaknesses) that make you less attractive to men. We call them "fatal flaws" because they typically are the dealbreakers in a relationship.

I remember going on a date with a guy a few years back, and during dinner, we really hit it off. He and I were getting along so well over the meal that we decided to go dancing afterwards. I am so glad we did! While we were dancing, this guy transformed into every song that the DJ played. Being a DJ myself, I've seen a lot of stuff on the dance floor, but nothing like this. When a Shabba Ranks song came on, he was Rastafarian. When a Beyonce song came up, he did booty dances like Beyonce. When a 50 Cent song came on, he marched around the floor like a wild thug. It was really freaky. I was spooked out and didn't know who this guy was; still, I knew that if he can change personalities that easily, he may have a few more personalities in there that I wouldn't want to meet. I left his butt on the dance floor and went home.

I have a cousin who I think is a walking poster of the worst fatal flaw that a woman can have: She's simply *crazy*. My cousin always finds herself destroying cars or starting fights in grocery stores. I don't really know how she became so mentally unstable, but she is simply nuts! Now many women in their right mind can be driven crazy on occasion because of the behavior or actions of a man. But it doesn't take much to make an unstable woman completely lose her mind. It's imperative to fix "crazy," through medicine or therapy. Forget about successful dating if you haven't fixed "crazy."

It is essential that you identify and fix your fatal flaws. Being single is a great time to fix your fatal flaws and improve yourself to attract new loves into your life. If you don't, they can cause men to miss or overlook so many of your wonderful positive traits. Some typical fatal flaws include body odor, bad skin, too much makeup, no manners/rudeness, a negative attitude, unkempt hair, just to name a few. I could go on, but you get the point.

Let's take one fatal flaw as an example, bad skin, which by the way is very fixable with a little effort. I know this because when I was in my early 20s I had horrible acne. A dermatologist tried many treatments like Retin-A, but my acne was ultimately resolved by Proactiv®. In my late 20s, I began to develop severe dry flaky skin. At that point, I had to research and understand what caused my dry skin and identify a facial moisturizer/cream that would resolve my problem. Due to these earlier challenges with my skin, I now invest time into my skincare with facials, moisturizers, and eye creams. Your face is your passport. Always aim to have clear, glowing healthy skin and be diligent about getting rid of bad skin.

It's important to note that it will not be an easy task to identify your fatal flaws. If they were easy to identify and fix, you probably would have done so by now. You will need to get honest feedback from your close family and trusted friends. Ask your family and close friends, "What's the worst personality trait I have?" If they love you, they will tell you. If they are honest and tell you some specific things, don't get mad; start working to improve them right away.

If you have a few close male friends, you could ask one of them what type of first impression you make to others. Men will typically tell you the truth, and they aren't as sensitive or worried as women are about hurting your feelings. And when they tell you, write down the exact words they use to describe you—both the positive and negative characteristics. This is about better understanding those areas in your life that you need to improve to attract more men into your life.

You could also notice what your friends and family say while joking or making fun of you. In their humor, you will get the truth. I have an uncle who tells you "the truth and nothing but the truth" when he's drinking. He once told me, "You are always broke. Why do you even go to work? You could stay at home all day and be broke too." I didn't realize that my finances were that bad, but I vowed to get myself financially stronger after he made that comment.

Even though we call them fatal flaws, sometimes it's the small things that turn off guys. Women who don't smile and have so much attitude can be a turnoff. I have a girlfriend who is famous for this. I remember one time in a restaurant a guy told her, "Smile girl... if the food is that bad, then you should return it."

If a man is originally attracted to you, he's going to either do one of two things. Be more attracted to you and want to see you more, or be less interested in you and want to see you less or even not at all. Be sure not to be fake and hide your fatal flaws; actually work towards fixing them so they won't become an issue later. A man will likely leave you, whether it's one week or one year into the relationship, if you have fatal flaws he cannot tolerate. Be sure to fix your fatal flaws so that you attract and keep men in your life.

Action Item:

Identify your Number One Fatal Flaw and make a conscious choice to fix it. Solicit input from family and friends if you cannot identify a fatal flaw on your own.

CHAPTER TEN

Have a Life of Your Own

I f you don't have a life of your own when you meet a man, you will quickly become clingy and desperate, and try to attach yourself to his life. It is important to have your own life because you don't want to expect a man to save you from yourself. He should just enhance your life. If you are waiting for a relationship to solve your financial or emotional issues, then you are relinquishing the responsibility for your happiness and fulfillment to someone else.

Dating a man is supposed to be fun and add to your life. It shouldn't become your whole life. Your first goal should be to improve your own life by becoming an independent, productive woman with goals, dreams and fulfilling activities. Women can afford to think more like men in this area. Instead of worrying about what he wants or what makes him happy, figure out what is going to make you happy. What are you really passionate about, and what do you enjoy doing? Do you have a rich social life with great friends and loving family members?

It's important to learn to be happy while you're single. Single women are beginning to realize that they actually have a lot of time to create a meaningful life for themselves, and they are deciding to pursue their dreams. Being single is not a problem, but an opportunity to reinvest in your life and your spiritual growth. Maximize your career, interests, hobbies and relationships while you're single, and make that time the best days of your life.

Many single women jump in and out of relationships because they don't want to be alone. There is a major difference between being "lonely" and "aloneness." Know that you may be alone, but you don't have to be lonely in life. Alone is defined as separate, apart, unique or unequaled. In contrast, being lonely is defined as lacking friendly companionship. If you have a full life of family, friends and dates, you don't have to lack companionship in your life and, therefore, you don't have to be lonely.

Being single and alone can be a wonderful experience. It's the perfect time for adventure, fun, romance, self-discovery and renewal. Before you get into a relationship, learn to be happy alone. Work on your personal happiness and enjoying the wonderful friends and family in your life.

In terms of work, make the most of your current job today. Find the sweet spot in your career, that place where your passion meets your talents. Always be excellent at what you do. When I worked at McDonald's as a teenager, I had the same work ethic then that I have today. I only earned $3.35 an hour but I worked hard for every cent. As a result of my hard work, I won a scholarship from McDonald's that paid for my first year in college. My advice is to maximize your job, no matter what it is. Be sure to show up on time, volunteer for assignments, become a problem-solver, and remain excellent at everything you do.

If you want to be a mom, don't obsess about having children. Stop listening to your biological clock, and start strengthening the family relationships that you currently have. Or if having a child is that important to you, consider options for being a single parent. For me, not having any children has caused me to have strong family ties with my mom, aunts, cousins, nieces and nephews. Even beyond your blood relatives, you can create an extended network of close personal friends, neighbors and co-workers.

One of the biggest secrets to attracting men is to have a full, active life. Ne-Yo, a popular R&B singer, has a song that is all about loving women who have their own thing going on. The song title is "Ms. Independent." By having your own life, you have something to bring to the relationship. You can add value to a man's life and become an asset to him.

Sometimes when we meet a new guy, we forget everything we did before we met him. We start canceling plans with family and friends, stop working out, quit hobbies, and try to keep our schedule open for whatever he wants to do. When you meet a new guy, don't lose the life you worked so hard to create. Keep active and don't become a slave to the telephone waiting for his call. Also, be sure that this romance is adding to your already full life, the one you've worked very hard to create.

Here are some ideas for making your life more full and productive:

- Get more education or finish a degree as this will enhance your career opportunities.

- Find another job that exploits your skills and abilities and increases your income. When we're in a relationship, we tend not to be as focused on work. However, when we're single, we can commit more time to our career or a new job.

- Work on your physical appearance and learn to maximize your best physical assets (more on this in the next chapter).

- Work on your emotional or mental health, particularly if you constantly deal with emotional issues such as insecurity, jealousy, or anger/rage.

- Go back to church to reconnect spiritually and study the Scriptures as they will speak to you and help guide you in life. When you study Scripture, focus on you; don't try to figure out what might help someone else.

- Participate in the community, or become a Big Sister (info at http://www.bbbs.org/) and role model for young adults. Kids today have a whole set of challenges that we didn't have growing up, and they could use our help.

Live a Life of Purpose

There has been a lot of emphasis in the last few years for people to live a life of purpose. I can understand why. As women, we go to work, help pay the bills, cook and clean the house, raise the children, but sometimes feel like there is more to life then the rut and routine we find ourselves in. Having a purpose gives our lives meaning, hope and significance.

Once you know the purpose for your life, you can determine how best to use your time on this earth. Purpose gives your life meaning and becomes the legacy of your life. For me, purpose provides a standard that helps when deciding which activities get my time and energy.

Have you ever known someone who is onto some new project or idea every time you see them? They're always bouncing around in life with no obvious direction or purpose. If I focus my time and energy on what is *truly important*, I can eliminate wasting time on things that will bring little results or satisfaction to my life. Ask yourself the following question: *What am I passionate about?* Do you have an answer? Having purpose in life produces passion. If I believe I am fulfilling my purpose, I will be passionate about what I am doing. You have to ask yourself, *"When this journey called 'life' is over, what type of legacy do I want to leave?"*

To help jumpstart your search for purpose, here are some suggestions that can help you answer the above questions:

- *Listen to your heart's desires.* We all have an inner voice that tells us our true desires. It will take practice to hear this voice but it will constantly remind you of what's important and what really makes you happy.

- *Embrace transformation.* Don't be afraid to change because it feels difficult or frightening. Change is a natural part of life.

- *Turn down the voices in the world.* Sometimes you have to go against the advice of family and friends. Be sure your voice is the strongest voice in your life.

- *Listen to your crisis.* Do you dislike your job? Is going to work stealing all your joy and energy in life? Do you have a hobby that makes you feel happy and fulfilled?

- *Forget your regrets.* Forget about mistakes you've made in the past or time wasted being unhappy or unfulfilled. Know that during that time you were gaining valuable life skills that will help you succeed today.

- *Have patience.* Be committed to finding your life's purpose in the small areas of your life. Don't expect grand changes overnight.

Once you begin living your life with passion, you'll want to reach your goals with everything in you, and you'll believe God has put you on earth to achieve those goals. Your vision will be so compelling that it will push you to take the necessary steps to move forward. Having a sense of purpose propels your dreams into action and motivates you to claim your destiny.

Action Item:

Create a statement of purpose for your life.
Write down what you believe you were put on
earth to be, do or accomplish.

Become an Interesting Person

Have you ever hung out with a dull person? Have you ever been the dull person on the date? Ask yourself, "How interesting am I?" When it comes to dating men, be sure to show many different sides of your personality so they don't become too bored with you. Our personality is the different ways we express ourselves.

Variety is the spice of life. Be an interesting Don't be a dull woman; have a sense of fun and a spirit to try new adventures. Long-term relationships and marriages can get dull and uninteresting very quickly, so don't allow them to fall into rut and routine. (Let me clarify something... When I write "become more interesting," which means be exciting, I'm not talking about creating chaos and unnecessary drama!)

One of the first things you have to do to become a more interesting person is to be interested in other people. If you have poor interpersonal skills or poor people skills, you will be less desirable to not only men, but to everyone and no one will want to spend time with you. Many women don't think about mastering their people skills as important when it comes to dating. But the success of any type of relationship is in how well you get along with people.

Let me add that having a sense of humor is very sexy and interesting. You don't have to be a stand-up comedian, but be funny, witty, light-hearted and don't take yourself too seriously. Also, don't become too predictable. Don't call him constantly or at the same time every day to check on him. Becoming too predictable is boring for anybody.

Action Item:

Identify three activities that you plan to do to make your life more rich, full and interesting.

CHAPTER ELEVEN

Begin Your Beauty Transformation

Most men may not admit this out loud, but a woman's looks are almost everything to a man. It is extremely important to him how attractive his lady is. Because men are visual creatures, they will initially be attracted to you by your physical appearance. A man must find something physically attractive about a woman for him to take interest in her.

Your physical appearance is an important asset. Men are attracted to beautiful women. There isn't a single man alive who can resist looking at attractive or sexy women. If you don't think you are beautiful or very attractive, no worries. Men are also attracted to passionate, confident women with a sense of style—all areas that can be developed and improved upon with focus and effort.

Your goal should be to look beautiful whenever you walk out the door. We have to realize that we are selling ourselves every time we are out and about in the world. Our appearance tells people about our age, profession, marital status, intelligence, and financial status. Even the style of your hair, or lack thereof, communicates a lot about you as well. Think of beauty as a method to create opportunities and options for you in your dating life.

It's important to know that not every guy will be interested in you no matter how pretty, sexy, smart and successful you are. Luckily for us, attractiveness comes in many colors, shapes and sizes because not all men are attracted to the same physical attributes. However, in general, men like the fact that a woman's body is physically different than theirs; they love the shapely curves of a woman.

Your beauty transformation is not about becoming drop-dead gorgeous, but it is about maximizing your physical beauty to the fullest. Your transformation is about making the most of whatever God has given you to work with and improving the aspects of your appearance that are within your control (weight, fitness, overall health, hair, skin, etc.). It is about dressing in a manner that allows you to show off your best assets, whether that be your legs, cleavage, butt, face or hair. I don't mean getting oversized boobs or other types of drastic cosmetic surgery, but maximizing your physical attributes/features to always look your best.

I know that you might be thinking, "If I dress like that, the only type of man who I will attract is one that wants to have sex with me." Well, that is true, but here is a newsflash: Men ask women out because they are physically or sexually attracted to her. Of course, he's asking you out because he wants to have sex with you. But that is the method for how to attract men. I don't understand it when women say that they want a man to love them for who they are. Well, of course, but they will never get to know who we are if they are not initially attracted or drawn to us. A man is not going to ask you out if he's not pleased with your physical appearance. If you don't attract him or get his attention, you'll never get a chance to share all the other wonderful aspects of your personality. The bottom line is that it's your exterior that gets his attention, and it is who you are on the inside that keeps him coming back for more.

So many beautiful women let themselves go and wonder why they have difficulty attracting men. One thing I learned about my mother is that she takes time to put herself together every day. I've always had her as a great role model. Every day she looks good. She puts on her make-up, jewelry, ironed clothing and makes sure she always looks great. When she is in pajamas, they would always be very classy and feminine.

Being attractive is not just about physical beauty, but also about having self-confidence in your ability to attract a man's attention. Being confident is contagious, and it's a major attraction factor. Once you maximize your physical beauty, be sure to have an air of self-confidence since you should be proud of how good you look. And let's not confuse confidence with arrogance. Arrogance is defined as an offensive display of superiority or self-importance. Arrogance causes people not to respect or like you, whereas confidence naturally draws people to you. Think and radiate beauty and love into the world, and it will return that to you.

My Beauty Transformation

As I discussed in greater detail earlier in the book, I recently completed a beauty transformation for myself, without the help of cosmetic surgery. I transformed myself with a total focus on outward beauty. I look at this beauty transformation as one of my highest accomplishments.

Highlights of some of the things that I did to maximize my physical appearance were:

- ✴ Hired a personal image consultant to help me enhance my best physical attributes and hide my flaws.

- ✴ Learned to dress for my body type by determining my specific body type out of 48 possibilities based upon height, weight and shape/contours. I also identified strategies for dressing sexy based upon my specific body type.

- ✴ Purchased attractive attire by upgrading my wardrobe to achieve a sexy and casual chic look with fitted jeans, sexy tops, and push-up bras.

- ✴ Upgraded my hairstyle with a new look that accented the shape of my face. I used weaves and extensions to make my hair longer and fuller with a layered cut.

- ✴ Received a face makeover to learn which foundation, shadows and blush colors looked best on my complexion to create a fresh, natural look.

- ✴ Developed a skin care routine to achieve a smooth, even complexion with a healthy glow to make my skin look youthful. I also learned that drinking lots of water, at least eight glasses per day, really helps the skin look beautiful.

- ✴ Reshaped my eyebrows to help define my entire face.

- ✴ Leveraged vitamins targeted to help my hair, skin and nails look healthier and grow faster.

Work It Out! Exercise Is Essential

For me, I dislike exercising more than anything else in the world. There's nothing more that I hate to do than exercise. But as I get older, I've found that I no longer have a choice. I have to exercise to stay fit and toned. However, I do love the results from exercising as I look and feel better with more energy and vitality. Although I am mentally committed to exercise, I struggle to keep the discipline required to maintain a regular exercise routine. I've even worked with personal trainers, on occasion, which helped me jumpstart my exercise routine. Once I established the routine, I could generally maintain it for three to four months at a time.

Exercising is essential. Be sure to do plenty of aerobic exercise because it's good for the heart. In terms of your beauty transformation purposes, it also causes you to sweat a lot. When you sweat, you release toxins that help to clear your skin. Always be sure to do abdominal exercises to achieve that flat stomach that men love. In addition, you want to use free weights to tone, and not bulk up. The goal is to look healthy, strong but still feminine. Also, the goal isn't to be paper thin, but to have a shapely, healthy body.

Workouts that have produced results for me in the past are Tae Bo® and Turbo Jam® because they are upbeat, fast and generate results. With those workouts, I got the cardio (aerobic exercise) along with the muscle toning and stretching. I also get to dance a bit, which is one of my most favorite things to do.

Over time, I get bored and have to mix up my exercise routine. For me, my striptease and pole dancing has provided the most effective workout that I have ever experienced. The pole requires significant arm strength because most of the time you are using your arms to lift your entire body. Your arms will get very strong. For my striptease class, the dips and gyrating leg movements have really toned up my thighs and legs.

I have even maintained a Vision Board to assist in my exercise goals. The Vision Board, which I learned about on Oprah's show about the book called *The Secret*, is a poster board on which you paste or collage images that you've torn out of various magazines. The idea is that you surround yourself with images and pictures of who you want to become, what you want to have, where you want to live, or where you want to vacation, and then your life changes to match those images and those desires. On my Vision Board, I have a picture of tone legs because that was one of my goals; achieving tone legs is really important to me.

To complement a solid exercise routine, you will need to maintain a healthy diet. This means eating well and maintaining a healthy weight long-term. Luckily, there has been significant information made available to us about dieting that works. Much of the teaching about eating good carbs vs. bad carbs has helped change the eating habits of many people with great success. Books like *The South Beach Diet* explain these concepts very well.

Start with a small workout and build up to a more difficult one. Ease into it. Increase your routine and continue to get to the next level of your workout. You may also need to get a workout buddy, someone you could go with and then you can keep each other accountable.

Today, I can honestly say that I'm in the best shape of my life. My butt is tight, my legs are toned, and I have more energy. My skin has a great glow as well. I love the feeling I have after I complete my workout. Upon completion, I think to myself, *you go girl*, and that usually sets me in the right direction for the rest of the day.

Action Item:

Develop a Beauty Transformation Plan that identifies specific things you can do to maximize your physical beauty.

CHAPTER TWELVE

Embrace Your Sexuality

Men are initially attracted to our sexiness and overall look. Other assets, such as intelligence, sweetness, good cooking, etc., are what keep him. However, he won't know about any of those assets if we don't initially get his attention. The women who leverage their best assets (i.e., the best features of their body) will have more choices in men.

Men will feel sexually attracted to you immediately or never. If they are attracted to you, they will become excited, nervous or simply turned on. I remember a guy walking over and telling me, "I've been watching you all night, and I have to admit that I have a crush on you." He said it in such a sincere and believable way, how could I not talk to him?

Embracing your sexuality means thinking of yourself as sexy and feeling that you are sexual regardless of whether or not you're about to have sex. It includes dressing and walking in a way that makes you feel sexy and confident. Every woman has a sexy feminine part of her that makes her most desirable to men, but sometimes we need to tap into it more. Are you confident, playful, sensual and mysterious when you interact with men? Do you accent the sexiest parts of your body when you dress, whether that be your breasts, butt, hair or legs? If your challenge is getting noticed when you walk into a room, then you should focus on enhancing your sexiness. Being sexy may not be the "thing" that he falls in love with; however, it is the "thing" that gets you noticed.

Suggestions for Embracing Your Sexuality

The following ideas will help you get in touch with your sexuality and discover your overall sexiness:

- ⚬ When you get dressed, always think sexy, then style. You want to look sexy but not sleazy. When you shop, achieve a sexy style that's perfect for your shape and body type.

- ⚬ Buy a new sexy top that tastefully shows cleavage. I assume you already have several push-up bras. Manageable cleavage is always sexy.

- ⚬ Accent your butt. Men love to see your booty; don't wear outfits that don't accent the shape of your butt. There are many jeans' guides that tell you how to buy jeans depending upon the shape of your hips and butt; this is an important detail to not overlook when shopping for jeans.

- ⚬ Become a great kisser and learn to enjoy it. People have forgotten how fun kissing can be. Kissing is sensual and is coming back in style!

- ⚬ Listen to music that makes you dance and feel good. (My favorite song that makes me feel sexy is Usher's "Bad Girl.") Another suggestion is to dance naked.

- ⚬ Get more comfortable with touching and being touched. You could begin by getting a full body massage to learn to appreciate the art of touching.

- Look men directly in the eye when you speak to them. This does not mean to stare, but to make solid eye contact.

- Watch romantic movies that spark romantic ideas and sayings.

- Take bubble baths with scented oils in the water and lit candles scattered about the room.

- Walk around the house naked or in front of the TV while he's watching it.

- Sleep in the nude or just in sexy underwear and no top.

- And my favorite, take a striptease class, which offers you the opportunity to really express your sexuality and simply feel sexier. There are studio classes, as well as DVDs (e.g., FlirtyGirlFitness™ DVDs at www.flirtygirlfit.com) that teach you how to striptease and get fit at the same time.

Learn to Flirt

Men really do love women who flirt. Flirting is being alluring in a playful manner. Flirting is playtime for adults, and it can be used as a tool for getting what you want from others (whether that be a date or a job promotion). Growing up as a tomboy, I would say that flirting is a new thing for me. However, I am starting to get the hang of it and never pass up an opportunity to flirt. Even if I'm bantering with a guy about sports, I flirt. Here are some tips for learning to flirt:

❧ First and foremost, be friendly and sweet when you flirt and keep it light-hearted. If you know you have a bad attitude that day, don't go out and flirt; it won't be effective.

❧ Look him directly in the eye and make eye contact with him. A woman's glance can be very powerful. It can be a very effective way to convey interest.

❧ Smile: If you smile, you show energy, enthusiasm and happiness, and everyone wants more happiness in their life. A smile lights up your face and lets others know that you're happy, approachable and enjoying your life. Also, be sure to get your teeth cleaned and whitened to have a sexy smile.

❧ Have a confident walk with good posture and grace. I don't mean you have to walk like you're on a runway, but be confident and easy in your walk with your shoulders tall and back. For me, this is a great challenge since I grew up as a tomboy; my walk isn't very sexy, but it is confident.

❧ When you apply lip gloss or lipstick, lick and wet your lips to smooth it out properly. My girlfriend did this while we were out one day, and a guy walked over and said, "What flavor is that lip gloss; you make me want to go out and buy some for myself."

❧ Most men will tell you that they like longer hair, and if you have it (whether it's yours or extensions), use it to your advantage. Try tossing or flipping your hair. More simply, you could run your fingers through your hair as well; it's seductive and ensures your hair maintains its body and fullness.

∞ If you're just learning to flirt, you may begin by walking up to a guy to ask him for help or advice. For instance, you could ask whether there is an ice cream shop nearby. It doesn't really matter what you ask him; you are learning to approach him and engage in a conversation with men.

I remember dating a younger guy who introduced me to a fun way to flirt with someone you're dating. This guy was about 10 years younger than me, so he was much savvier with texting or "sexting." He taught me how to take pictures of myself and send them via my phone. Depending on your age range, you may have very different views of this. If you're under 35 years old, you're thinking, "This is nothing new. I've been texting seductive pics to my man for years." If you're over 35 years old, you're thinking, "I would never do that. This sounds like letting a man videotape you during sex." However, it is different than that, and it can be very entertaining. The original guy who gave me this idea would ask me to send him pics of different parts of my body. At first, I said, "No way!" But then after he sent me a few, I realized how much I enjoyed receiving them from him. If you do plan to send sexy pics by phone or email, never include your face. You wouldn't want them to end up on the Internet. Still, that is a small risk that you take.

Understanding the Power and Pleasure of Sex

I believe that sex is one of the greatest and most powerful experiences on earth. As I mentioned earlier, the vagina is a tool of female empowerment.

Ladies, it is time to reconnect with our sexual selves! Don't blame others for your lack of sexual desire and interests. Take the responsibility to discover what pleases you sexually. You have to be comfortable with your sexuality in order to please a man and meet his needs. Men are drawn to women who are comfortable with their sexual identity. So why not maintain a healthy view of sex and be open to new experiences? However, keep in mind that most men are generally freaky, and I would never suggest you do everything freaky with a man who won't even do the small things for you—such as taking you out to a nice dinner on occasion.

Men love sex! And they actually need sex physically, for the physical sexual release it provides. Men will also use women for sex. Men can have sex with women they have no feelings for whatsoever. One of my guy friends has this prioritized list of women he has sex with, and sometimes when we're out, he's seeking to add to his list and plans to drop some others off the list. I often call him "immature"; however, he says, "The women know about my list, and they don't care so why should you?" I said, "Good point!"

If you generally have a low sex drive and are not interested in sex, you may want to seek a doctor to see what's causing it. Sometimes, it is due to being tired or stressed, but it may be physical and due to a hormonal imbalance. Whatever the reason, if you still don't seem to be interested in sex, you may want to try some natural herbals or supplements to help increase your sex drive. There are also topical treatments, such as Vazoplex (http://www.vazoplex.com). I know that Vazoplex is simple and easy to use; you just apply a small amount with your fingertip and your man would never know it's there because it will feel like natural moisture to him.

There is a difference between good sex and great sex for a man. That difference is determined in part by your pleasure. Men want to please women in bed and be certain that their sex partner is satisfied. It really turns him on to know that he can please you, bring you to an orgasm, and satisfy you. For this reason and for your own pleasure, you'll want to be able to sincerely enjoy and receive enjoyment from sex.

Sexual compatibility is a necessary part of a meaningful relationship. And even if you think you have the "good good" when it comes to sex, it is just one of the keys to intimacy. Sex alone will not make a man want to marry you. Maybe sex and a beautiful face and body, but good sex alone is usually not enough for a man to want to make a marital commitment. However, bad sex will definitely cause him to seek sex from someone else.

Don't underestimate the importance of sex in a relationship. Seek to keep the spice and spark in your sex life.

Action Item:

Identify three specific things you will do to become more sexy and flirtatious.

CHAPTER THIRTEEN

Two Necessities –
A Good Job and Good Credit

L et's face it; success is sexy. I have always been attracted to successful, powerful men like Jared Ashton, my corporate model of success. And for me, my best chance to attract Jared was to become as successful and powerful in my own career. Throughout my career, I've focused on success and money. I didn't just want the promotion; I made sure that the money came along with the advancement. I used to tell my manager, "Don't give me an award or certificate, unless a bonus is attached to it." I wasn't being ungrateful; money is how value is determined in business. *My attitude is: If I'm as valuable as you say that I am, then pay me.*

If you're not financially independent and you totally depend on a man, you will have fewer options in life. My advice is to be sure you maintain your financial independence. When I speak of financial independence, I don't necessarily mean being rich, but rather having the ability to take care of yourself and buy what you want and need. Many years ago, women were not afforded similar opportunities as men in the business world; the only way women could get financial security was through inheritance or marriage. However, in this day and age, we have access to more opportunities for financial independence.

I must admit that I've always been challenged by my relationship with money. I have spent more than I earned, never balanced a checkbook, kept my credit cards maxed out, and lived with no savings. All of these are things a financial planner would tell you not to do. All the signs made me realize I needed to re-examine my relationship with money and learn how to improve my financial stability. Even today, I could still do a much better job of managing my financial life. As a result, I have hired financial planners and accountants to work with me and provide assistance in this area because I understand the importance of financial independence. I would also recommend Suze Orman's books for more expert advice on personal finance.

It requires a lot of self-discipline to set and achieve financial goals. It is very important to write down your financial goals so you can create a budget for spending, saving and investing to ensure that you can achieve those goals. Typical goals include purchasing a home, buying a new car, eliminating credit card debt, or saving for your child's college education. Many people, including myself, find it hard to develop and maintain a budget. Your budget is your short-term spending plan, which is the foundation for managing your income and expenses to attain your financial goals.

Additionally, many people do not know their own net worth, which gives you a look at your financial strength. If you work with a financial planner, they will help you do this. If you want to get a quick snapshot of your net worth today, you can do this simple task. Add up all of your assets, and subtract all of your debts from your total assets. Your assets include cash, stocks, house equity, and the cars and trucks that you own, and debts include credit cards, mortgage debt, installment loans, etc. This will give you a quick look at your current net worth, and of course, the higher the number (assuming your assets outweigh your debts), the better.

Leverage Your Good Job to Gain Financial Stability

Financial stability means earning a good income, having savings, good credit, and long-term financial plans. If you get your finances in order before you meet a man, you'll have something to bring to the relationship, besides debt. Together, your combined financial portfolio will be a lot stronger. He'll feel that you are an asset and not a burden to him. Otherwise, he could even begin to lose respect for you for not contributing financially or bringing anything to the table.

I had a cousin who owned a business, and she let her relationship with her boyfriend (not husband) limit her ability to grow her business. I never understood why she would do that. Her boyfriend worked part-time and could barely afford to pay his bills, much less her bills. Never let a man limit your ability to achieve your financial goals. I know I had to learn this lesson the hard way, but I never let a man mess with my money now.

Having strong financial health is critical. For a single woman, her happiness depends on whether she can carry herself financially and do the things she wants to do. This significantly affects her quality of life in terms of where she can live, what she can buy, where she can travel to, etc. The reality is that in today's competitive dating world, you will need to invest time and money into maximizing your physical appearance—whether that is for hair and nail care, a gym membership or personal trainers, sexy attire, shoes, handbags, facials or spa treatments. Your income must allow you to cover some of the major expenses associated with looking beautiful.

Establish Good Credit

One of your financial goals should be to have excellent credit. You should relentlessly pursue your goal to have perfect credit until you achieve it. Having an excellent credit score is much better than having cash in the bank because it gives you access to cash and large purchases. Some jobs even check your credit report and use that to evaluate your candidacy with their company.

What's considered a good credit score? Your credit score can range from 300 to 850. Lenders will generally give you a car or home loan for credit scores above 600. However, the golden score is considered to be above 720. A score higher than 720 is the magic number for getting the best loans.

Here are some tips for improving and better leveraging your credit score:

Know your credit score:

Many people don't know what their credit score is. To find out, get your credit scores from all three credit bureaus—Trans Union, Experian and Equifax. Your credit score, also called your FICO score, is the system lenders use to determine if you are a credit risk. With a poor credit score, you may not be able to get loans, or may get higher than the average loan rates due to a less than stellar credit score. The quickest way to get your credit score online is through each credit bureau or MYFico.com.

Dispute all derogatory items:

Some credit repair companies will charge you hundreds of dollars to fix your credit, but what they're actually doing is just disputing derogatory items. However, you can dispute these derogatory items yourself. Things like repossessions, bankruptcies, charge-offs, liens, collections, and other derogatory information can all come off your credit report via a "dispute." In some cases, the derogatory item is actually inaccurate, and you definitely don't deserve to have anything on your report that is wrong. Your creditor is required by law to verify items and report back to the credit bureau within 30 days. If they find the item is old or inaccurate, they will tell the credit bureau and your item will be deleted. Keep in mind that each deletion can increase your credit score by 20-25 points, so these deletions are very important to improving your credit score. Be prepared to prove that the item is inaccurate, by showing a canceled check for payment for instance. Sometimes the item is accurate but it still gets deleted anyway. This can happen for several reasons:

- *The creditor has received payment and does not care to respond to the dispute from the credit bureau.* Then the item gets deleted because the creditor didn't respond within the 30-day timeframe. Sometimes the creditor simply does not try to prove the item is accurate, because they have already been paid for it.

- *Some collection agencies will delete items that have been paid, if you ask them "Do you delete?"* If they do delete, it may be for a nominal fee, but this is still worth it so that the deletion can increase your credit score.

- You can also dispute your high credit card balances. Sometimes the loan balance data at the credit bureaus is as much as six months old, so that may limit your ability to qualify for loans due to high balances.

Reduce high balances on unsecured debt:

Your credit report doesn't tell a lender how much you earn, but it does tell them about your ability to repay a loan. However, being "maxed out" on your credit cards is a sign that your spending may be exceeding your income, which is a possible sign of future credit problems. If you have high balances on your credit cards, this will negatively impact your credit score. As far as calculating your credit score, having high credit card balances account for about 35% of a low credit score. The goal should be to keep your credit card balances between 30-40% below the credit card limit. You could also consolidate your debt onto one lower interest card.

Limit the number of inquiries:

There are no negative consequences if you pull your credit report yourself. However, if any mortgage lender, credit card company, or any other type of creditor pulls your credit report, it counts against you as an "inquiry" and counts against your credit score. Inquiries stay on your credit reports for two years, and are difficult to get removed.

Pay attention to the middle score:

Nowadays, mortgage lenders are using third party credit reporting agencies that provide all three of your credit reports, which give the mortgage lenders three different scores. The mortgage lenders will look at and determine your credit risk based on the middle score. For example, on TransUnion, you have a 620, on Experian you have a 700, and on Equifax, you have a 724. Therefore Experian has the middle score that will be used to determine your credit worthiness. You could focus on raising the scores of the two highest scores so that you best focus your efforts.

Know in advance which credit bureau a lender (e.g., car dealer) uses:

If you know which credit bureau has your highest credit score, use those car dealerships to purchase your car. You can easily call a car dealer and ask. Then use that dealer who pulls the credit report with your best score to get a better loan.

Taking control of your financial life will benefit you in so many ways. As we discovered earlier, you have a better chance of attracting a mate with certain traits if you have those same traits yourself. If you're interested in a man with money, then work on being financially strong and independent. There are many powerful men who are suspicious of women being just interested in them for their money. However, if your life is full and financially stable, he would look at you as being more compatible with him.

In summary, financial independence helps a woman become more powerful. Being powerful as a woman is not just about having money, but rather it's about being comfortable and confident in who you are and what you contribute to the world. Be confident that people will want to spend time with you because you have something of value to offer. If you've completed your Relationship Market Value assessment (see Chapter 8), you now have better clarity on the value you bring to a romantic relationship.

Action Item:

Take the time to assess your overall financial health and credit worthiness. Work to increase your credit score, increase your savings, and manage money more wisely.

CHAPTER FOURTEEN

Expand Your Circle of Friends, Hang Out with Guys and Learn from Divas

Women need to hang out with men to understand men. So why not start hanging out with guys? If you spend time around men and observe their behavior, you'll have a much better idea of what they think about women. This will help you better understand what's going on when you are interacting with a man and getting to know him. As an example, if you want to know what men find sexy in women, read the sexy magazines that guys read, such as *Playboy*, *Maxim* and *King*. Also, try to get immersed in guy things, such as sports and cars. This will help you engage with a man when you're getting to know him. This is easy for me since I am an avid sports fan and I love fast sports cars. I am genuinely interested in some of the same things guys are. I grew up with three brothers, and since we only had one TV to watch, my mom would make us vote on what we were going to watch for the evening. You can probably guess that we watched sports most of the time. Now today I love sports, and one of my favorite things to do is to watch a football or basketball game. When my TV is on, nine times out of ten, I am watching ESPN.

Look at the Quality of Your Current Female Friendships

Evaluate the girlfriends you hang out with today. We all need them for the support and wisdom they share. However, not all of them are in your corner. There always seem to be those who bring you down or constantly try to bring your man down. They live with a lot of drama and always want to bring drama into your life.

Additionally, are you hanging out with women who have similar aspirations in life? Are they positive and encouraging? Are they dating quality men? It's ok to let go of female friends who don't help lift you up in life. Having good female friends is valuable if they share desires and dreams similar to yours. If they support you and provide constructive feedback to help you grow, those relationships can be invaluable. That strong circle of friends can feel good and bring enjoyment to your life. Female friends are fun, but be sure those relationships are healthy.

My closest female friends are my cousins, who are really like my sisters. My best girlfriend Barbara has been my closest female friend for over 20 years. I have to admit, I have more male friends than women friends. However, I do value the women friends who are in my life, and I consider them to be of the highest quality.

"Hanging Out" with a Group of Women Limits Your Ability to Meet Men

If you want to have a girls night out, by all means do so, and enjoy the company of your sisters. But you should limit the number of women you hang out with in one setting when you want to meet new men. The number one reason for this is that men will be less inclined to approach you if you're with a larger group. Men have a fear of being rejected, and it's even worse to be rejected in front of several women. Try to hang out with one woman at best when you're "man hunting," and even if you do hang out with one woman, don't stay glued to her all night. Just plan on connecting at a pre-arranged time but mingle alone. You will be much more approachable to men if you are by yourself. If you are out to meet men with a bunch of women, free yourself from the pack, be confident and go mingle alone. Give this strategy a try, and I think you'll see that it increases the number of men you meet while you're out.

Additionally, maybe you have a girlfriend who you've come to know, and you realize that she is a little strange. Please spend quality time with her in your girls' one-on-one time, like when you're going to the mall. Odd women really turn men off, and everyone else for that matter. They dress bad when they hang out, they diss a man every time he opens his mouth, or they sit at a table and play games on their phone the whole time you're out. These women are challenged interpersonally, and they need to work on their social skills before they're ready to hang out and meet guys with you.

One other note regarding girlfriends. I assume that women already know not to discuss their sex life with other women or girlfriends. If not, I would highly recommend that you be extremely discreet about the intimate details of your relationship. You would never want something negative you said to get back to your guy. Also, with this dating environment being so competitive, what's to gain by telling your single girlfriend how great your man is in bed. I'd recommend maintaining your privacy and discretion in your intimate relationships.

Learn from Divas

There's a Beyoncé song that talks about divas being the female version of a hustler. Divas have much game and they know it. They are incredibly confident, with a sex appeal and a great look. Here are their characteristics:

- Divas dress sexy with a great sense of style. All men notice these women when they walk into the room.

- They are sexual and don't apologize about it.

- A diva gets and understands how men think and what men want.

- They've mastered the art of flirting and communicate with their eyes to first get a man's attention.

- They can become uninterested in a guy and cut him off without thinking twice because they know there are more out there.

- They hang out with men and have just a few female friends.

My suggestion would be if you know a Diva, hang with her, if she lets you, and learn some of her secrets.

Action Item:

List three male heterosexual friends who you currently have and work to develop those friendships. If you don't have any male friends, then begin by developing a relationship with one guy who can just be your pal.

CHAPTER FIFTEEN

Decide Whether to Accept a Role in His Life

While dating a man, there are many different roles that we can play. However, most of us end up playing the role that he chooses for us. It is time that we take control of our dating life and decide if we want to be in his life. Instead of trying to make the relationship something it is never gonna be, you decide if the role he wants you to play is acceptable to you. If he just wants to be pals or for you to be his Jump-Off, determine if that role is right for you and meets your needs at that particular time in your life. If not, quickly move on to the next guy. Trying to make a relationship something it's not is a waste of time.

Having played all of the roles below, sometimes unknowingly, I've learned that there are very distinct characteristics of each relationship that will help you determine the role he wants you to play. Most of the time, a man will not come right out and say, so you will have to notice the clues below. Only you should decide if you want to play that role and continue in the relationship with him.

Here are the Roles of a Dating Relationship:

Hottie/Trophy:

This is when he dates you solely based upon your looks and sexiness. This is the sexy woman who is desirable to the majority of men. If you check out a *Playboy*, *Maxim* or *King* magazine, that will give you a good idea of what most men find sexy. The better you look, the more dates you will get. This woman has no trouble getting phone numbers or dates, but many of these relationships are not deep or committed. The reason for this is that the guy's primary interest in her is how she looks. However, she gets much attention and is asked out frequently. If dating is truly fun to you and you enjoy the sport of dating, you will take pride in being his Hottie/Trophy.

Homie/Friend (Pal):

This is when the guy is not interested in you physically, but thinks that you are kinda cool to hang out with (they feel like you are one of the fellas). You have to ask yourself, "Does it make sense to just be his friend?" I say yes, because these relationships are important; you need male friends to really get to know men. If you want advice on becoming more attractive to men, a close male friend can give you the best feedback and advice. By hanging out with male friends, you will hear the things they say about women, and learn how they approach ladies. I think some of the comments men say about women are just fascinating. I recommend that you have no less than three male heterosexual friends that you can just hang out with. I'm a big sports fan, and I love to hang out in sports bars with my male friends. I am always amazed at their conversation; things that are not appropriate to say in this book. I wouldn't recommend these relationships become sexual; if they do, and he only looks at you as his Buddy, then you still may not become Wifey material to him. You just become his "Homie-Lover-Friend."

Booty Call/Jump-Off:

This is the woman that the guy uses only for sex and other sexual pleasures. She is usually available anytime and anyplace for any type of sexual encounter. This is the woman he goes to for that three-some or some late night head after the club. When Wifey or Girlfriend is getting on his nerves, the Booty Call/Jump-Off is usually the one to hold him over for a few hours. The Jump-Off will typically never hear from the man unless he wants sex.

- The Booty Call can have its benefits if you're not trying to make the relationship something it's not. It is not hard to figure out if this is the type of relationship he wants from you. If the only time you hear from him is to have sex, then you're not "dating" him; it is a Booty Call, which is an appointment to have sex. In fact, if the only way he communicates with you is by text message, you just might be his Jump-Off.

- I'm not here to pass judgment on this type of relationship. My point is that you decide if you want to be his jump-off or not. You decide what's best for you at a particular time in your life. I know a lot of ladies, including me, wouldn't mind being Jamie Foxx's jump-off. Just kidding!

129

Mistress/The Other Woman:

The Mistress is his woman, who is usually as sexy or nice-looking as Wifey/Girlfriend, but he feels she is somewhat replaceable. She often thinks she's going to be the next Wifey/Girlfriend since she gets some similar benefits of a Wifey—quality time every now and then, presents on birthdays and holidays, plus vacations. The Other Woman can be a real threat to Wifey; if things with Wifey go bad, the Mistress can step into her place rather quickly, as she has an emotional relationship with him as well. Even though the Mistress is attached emotionally to the man, she does a great job keeping their relationship private, sometimes for years at a time.

Wifey/Girlfriend:

Since the Wifey/Girlfriend role is the end goal for many of us, I will spend more time on this role. The Wifey/Girlfriend is that role reserved for the one person he feels is irreplaceable in his life. Wifey/Girlfriend is the sexiest, most successful, and most respected of all the women. She is loved, needed and wanted by her man. She is the woman that a guy will love and will always love, and he never wants to see her with another man. He may even show public displays of affection with her.

- He respects her, either her talents, knowledge, faith or something else beyond how she looks. He generally respects and admires many aspects of her persona.

- These women are often sweet and kind. They soften a man and allow him to be masculine. They are warm, kind and bring peace to his life. They generally are understanding and supportive in his life's endeavors and she is the first to hear of important news in his life. She can cook and keeps a clean house, a place he can call home.

- These women become his best friend. They have common interests, goals, desires and values. Most important, she goes home to meet his mom and other family members. She fits into his social lifestyle, but is also very independent and has a full life as well.

- Here are some signs to know if he sees you as Wifey/Girlfriend material:

  * He wants to spend significant time with you.
  * He seeks your opinion and approval on things that matter to him.
  * He introduces you to his mom, family, friends and co-workers.
  * His sexual interest is generally always there.
  * He leaves you alone at his place or leaves his phone unattended.
  * He falls asleep cuddling you.
  * He enjoys looking at photos of you.
  * He'll call you several times throughout the day, just to chat or check in.
  * It's difficult for him to say no to you.
  * He'll ask you on a date and spend time with you outside of the house.
  * He introduces you as his woman.
  * He attends a wedding or funeral (emotionally charged events) with you.

Knowing the role we play in the dating relationship is empowering because it is about taking control of our dating life and making decisions that are best for us. Remember, trying to make a relationship something that it is not is a waste of time.

Action Item:

Think about the guy(s) you currently date. Determine what type of dating relationship you have, and you decide if that role is right for you at this time in your life.

PART III

THE DATING
ACTION PLAN:

*Find the Man
that Every Woman Wants*

THE DATING ACTION PLAN:

Find the Man that Every Woman Wants

Sometimes it's hard to determine if a man is right for you. Or maybe your intuition tells you that he's not right, but you stay in the relationship and desperately try to make it work.

In this section, you'll learn how to identify a mate who is the right match. In this process, it is important to understand that men think very differently than women about sex, dating and relationships. You'll learn how men think, which can greatly increase your odds of finding the right guy.

Who is that man that every woman wants? Here are some of the ideal characteristics that women point out:

* This man absolutely loves women, and he is genuinely interested in them (their bodies, moods, hopes, and what makes them laugh).

* He is financially stable and career-minded.

* He's God-fearing with integrity and values.

* He's charming, funny and interesting.

* The guy has a great body, and if he's not physically fit, he carries his weight well in how he dresses.

✗ He has many female friends from all walks of life, and he has remained friends with most of his ex-girlfriends.

✗ This man is great in bed, and he helps us express our fantasies and more freely enjoy sex.

✗ He nourishes our spirit.

✗ He appreciates women and compliments them for their beauty.

Wouldn't you love to come across a man like this? Well, finding the right man will require deliberate planning and strategizing to proactively meet potential men who could be ideal for you. Keep reading!

CHAPTER SIXTEEN

Steer Clear of Unavailable Men

When dating, there are certain relationships that are harmful and downright dangerous. These are relationships with unavailable men—the men who are not available or ready to have a meaningful relationship with a woman. This type of relationship has very little chance of long-term success. Many older wiser women have already been down this road, and they know better than to get involved with an unavailable man. As a result, this advice is generally geared for younger women.

Here are the Types of Unavailable Men:

Addicts

Addicts are men with destructive personal habits, such as chronic alcohol, drug or gambling problems. Personally, a guy who drinks or smokes doesn't bother me too much as I grew up around relatives who were casual drinkers and smokers. However, what I'm referring to here is the chronic abuser, cases where their addictions cause them to lose their jobs, homes and sometimes family and friends.

I remember a cousin telling me about a guy she was seeing who had a drinking problem. He would get drunk on Friday through Sunday and become a terror; and Monday through Thursday, he would not have any drinks at all and became an upstanding citizen. Monday through Thursday, he just went to work everyday and was a mild-mannered guy. However, when he drank on weekends, this man couldn't control himself. He was like the Incredible Hulk. He would beat my cousin, fight with her, and curse her. Even if she threw grits or boiling hot water on him, the guy still came at her. After about a year of that, she decided to defend herself and purchased a gun. This unfortunately resulted in him being shot by her. But defend herself she did. After that, my cousin and her kids were safe as he never came back or harassed them again. Dealing with someone with a chronic addiction can be dangerous or even deadly. You cannot change him. Only God can do that, and the man has to commit to changing his life for himself.

Homosexuals/Bi-Sexual Men

Recently there has been a trend of down-low men coming out of the closet. These are men who are married or in committed relationships with women, but they also have sex with men. In other words, they have a gay side to them. Don't let these men fool you, even if he says he only did it once or twice. A man who is attracted to men will likely always be attracted to men. This could be an ongoing part of your bisexual man's lifestyle. I do recognize that some women have no issues with dating bi-sexual men; however, for many of us, we'd rather not be in a relationship with a bi-sexual man.

Some women knowingly are involved with gay men with hopes that these men will decide they are not gay and will fall in love with them. These guys make great friends, especially for shopping or the movies, but they may not be a great candidate for love. According to his own nature, a gay man will desire to be intimate with other men. Don't fool yourself into thinking you can love him straight (to become a heterosexual man).

The Always Unemployed Man

Anyone could go through hard times, but there are some guys who are never seriously looking for a job. They want or expect their mother or girlfriend to help pay their way. If a man doesn't have a job but he has skills and is seriously looking for work, then helping out is understandable. However, consider this… I know this one guy who allows women to pay his way because he can't find a job in his chosen field. After a year, it seems as though he would find other work to create some income for himself, but instead he continues to rely on women to foot the bill. I can't blame a man if a woman is comfortable paying all of his bills; to each its own.

Be very careful about paying a man's way; there are some men who are con artists and spend their whole life getting over on people. You may just be his next victim. If you dip into your life-savings to help him because he said he will pay you back when he gets on his feet, I would be extremely careful. I would recommend that you never do this; but if you do, at least get a promissory note so you have some legal means to get your money back if need be. For a relationship to survive and be balanced, it is helpful if a man is gainfully employed.

Playas (Players)

He's smooth and at ease with women. He generally

dresses well, has nice cars, and looks good all the time, as this helps him attract more women. However, he thrives on the chase, the thrill of getting more women in bed. For as much interest he showed in you initially, that will fade once you have sex with him. At that point, he's generally less interested and often becomes cold and distant. He is famous for saying, "I'll call you," but he rarely does.

Here are the characteristics of a playa:

- Likes to get women in bed and have many conquests, and he keeps count.
- Dates women for sport or for the conquests, more than for the love of women.
- Hangs out with lots of other guys.
- Uses props (fancy cars or watches) to get women.
- Brags to others about who/when/where and how many women he has sex with.

Abusers

He is physically or emotionally abusive towards women. You can sometimes find out about this type of guy by doing an online background check. If he has a criminal record for abusive behavior, it will be available as a public record.

How to Tell If He's an Unavailable Man

It is important to determine if a guy is unavailable before you get involved in a serious relationship with him. A woman's intuition will generally give her clues that a man is unavailable for a meaningful relationship; however, if you need some more concrete ways to determine this, see the list below:

- **He can never answer his phone around you.**
When I was younger, I had a boyfriend who used to
always answer his phone when we were together.
One day when I was visiting with my aunt, I told her
about how his phone was always ringing. My aunt
said, "Don't worry about that; worry when he doesn't
answer his phone around you." I thought to myself,
Good point!

- **He constantly borrows money from you and
everyone in his family.** He also never keeps a job
or is always between jobs. If he is frequently getting
fired from a job, that is a very bad sign!

- **He wants to spend time at your place only.** This
means he either lives with someone or never knows
when a woman could come knocking at his door. He
may also want to hang out at your place instead of
going out in public for fear of being seen with you.

- **He is inconsistent about when he calls and sees
you.** He also has sex with you less and less. If a
man's sex drive drops off significantly, he could be
having sex with someone else. One of my girlfriends
always kept count of her boyfriend's condom supply
and used that to measure if he was sleeping with
someone else. I wondered why she just never asked
him if he was cheating.

- **He can never be definitive about making plans or
is constantly canceling.** This is my pet peeve. If a
man needs to keep his plans open (in case something
better comes along), then I'm not interested in a date
with him. I remember once a guy canceled our date,

if you want to call what he did "canceling a date" (keep reading!). The plan was for me to cook his favorite meal, pork chops and gravy, with no mush-rooms, and after I toiled away in the kitchen for two hours, our plans were canceled at the last minute. And to keep it real, the man was late and I had to call to see where he was, and that's when he said he wasn't going to make it; I'm not sure if that qualifies as him "canceling the date." I've always wondered, if I didn't call him, would he have been considerate enough to call to cancel? I will never know and I never cooked for him again.

• **He stops bringing you around family and friends.** This is because he is afraid his simple friends will accidentally blow his cover. I actually did that to a guy friend of mine. Not on purpose, of course. But I told the woman he was with, "You look so different from when we hung out last week but maybe it was the lighting in the restaurant?" The woman said, "I've never met you before." I said, "My mistake... maybe it was someone else!" This guy was always trying to get over on women.

Action Item:

If you've just discovered that you are dating an unavailable man, it's likely that you should work on getting out of that relationship as quickly as possible.

CHAPTER SEVENTEEN

Determine His Value to You

Each man has a price tag or some value or worth to you. When you're in a relationship, you must ask yourself, "What's in it for me?" Can you clearly articulate what you're getting out of the relationship? If you cannot, then you may be in the relationship to please him or someone in your family, when you're really not getting what you need and want from a relationship.

It is important to know what you want from a man or a relationship. If you don't know, then your chances are poor of ever getting it. When you know what you want and value in a mate, you can do the choosing opposed to waiting to be chosen. Choosers know what they want and take responsibility for getting it. You are in charge of creating the love life that you want. Know what you want and take the initiative to go after it!

So many women go into a relationship without a wish list of what they are looking for in a man. You have to be clear on what you're looking for. If you went to buy a car, you would have an idea of what type of car (sedan, mini-van, convertible, SUV) as well as the price range you were willing to pay. If not, the dealer could easily sell you on a two-door, two-seat convertible for you and your three kids. Decide what you want in a man before you go searching for a mate.

Imagine or identify the things that you really admire and appreciate in men. Many of the desired physical and material attributes are the same for most women. They'd like a guy who is good-looking or handsome, and someone who is financially stable or well off. I've yet to hear any woman say they were looking for an unattractive, poor man. What I'm asking is that you look deeper to identify your particular wants and needs, that way you can seek the compatibility needed for a deeper, more fulfilling relationship.

Important note: Get to know the difference between a dating relationship and a long-term committed relationship. If we want to have dating relationships for fun and recreation, we will need to stop trying to make every guy we date our husband or our long-term committed partner. We can simply have fun and enjoy a man's company. Since the process of dating does not have to end in a marriage, we have to be able to quickly discern whether a man is a potential good partner for dating versus someone who is a good life partner or husband.

Don't make the mistake others have made by having so much fun dating that you assume a long-term committed marriage is the likely next step. Just because the two of you are having a great time dating doesn't necessarily mean you will be successful in a long-term committed relationship. Knowing what you need in an ideal mate for a long-term committed relationship has to be very clear in your mind.

Developing the List

How do you identify the qualities you like in that special man? First, think of the men you admire and respect.

Also, listed below are some questions that should help you create your list. Use these questions to create a list of characteristics and traits you want in an ideal mate. The purpose of the list is to help you clearly define what is best for you based upon your needs, wants and desires. Be sure to be as specific as possible. Only think about what you want or desire, not what someone else wants for you. No matter how small or trivial the trait seems, write it down if it matters to you.

* What are his physical attributes (height, complexion, body type)?

* What is his age range (e.g., 30 and over)?

* Is he honest and have integrity, or should you count on the occasional white lie?

* What is his personal style? How does he dress?

* Is he a professional or hard-working blue collar type?

* Is he shy or outgoing?

* Is he smart (book smart or college-educated)?

* Would he have a high sex drive or no sex drive?

* Is he financially stable or living paycheck to paycheck?

* Does he have a 401(k) or does he even know what a 401(k) is?

* Does he have a sense of humor or does he take himself way too seriously?

* Does he have good credit or does he not even know what his credit score is?

145

* Is he athletic or fit, and if not, does he look good in his clothes?

* Does he love God and attend regular church services?

* Does he have kids, and if he does, has he been spending time with them?

* Does he have ambition and career aspirations?

* Is he good in bed or clueless in terms of pleasing a woman?

* Is he secretive and prone to lying?

* Does he have good social skills or can he never attend a corporate function with you?

* Does he participate in volunteer, community or charity events?

* Does he like animals, and if so, which ones?

* Is he family-minded, and does he have strong family ties?

* Is he adventurous and like to try and see new things? Does he like to travel?

* Is he politically aware or politically active?

* Is he a homebody, or does he have to be at every hot party, club or movie opening?

* Does he drink or smoke? If so, how much and what is he drinking and smoking?

How to Use the List

Now that you've completed the list, indicate which characteristics are "Must Haves" and which ones are "Nice to Haves." The "Must Haves" are non-negotiable characteristics that you absolutely require in a man; they are the things that are required or the relationship simply will not work. On the other hand, the "Nice to Haves" are things that you are willing to compromise on. Your list of both types of items will ensure that you maintain the right focus when you date. That is, that you can begin to start choosing your mates, as opposed to waiting to be chosen by the men.

Once you create your list, keep the reversed 80/20 Rule in mind. This means that if you find 80% of what you're looking for, don't worry about the 20%. If he has the majority of the qualities you want and he truly makes you happy, compromise on the 20% and enjoy him for who he is. Unless there are some non-negotiable qualities you've discovered along with the 80% you want, work toward building a meaningful relationship. In contrast, if you meet a guy with very few of the qualities or traits you're looking for, please don't waste time trying to change him for a serious relationship. You will only frustrate yourself. Men really do not want to be changed by women.

Your list will be a living document. Please review the list often and make edits as necessary. As you mature and grow, your wants and needs may change, and you'll discover new characteristics that you want in a mate. Feel free to edit your list over time. This list is key to keeping your love life on track; every time you meet a new guy, you should assess his value to you based upon how well he matches the characteristics on your list. It will also help you prioritize how much time to give him based upon his value to you.

An important note about the list: If you have been attracting men who don't match many of the characteristics on the list, then you may have to look at the "woman in the mirror." We really tend to attract people who are very similar to us. To attract a man who has the qualities on your list, you must possess those qualities in yourself first. As an example, if you're looking for a man who is highly educated, but you only finished high school, enroll in college courses and get your degree. If you want an athletic, fit guy, but you haven't exercised in over 10 years, you're not likely going to attract that type of fellow. He will likely prefer a woman who is athletic and fit since that is something he values in his own life. My point is that you need to work on possessing the characteristics that you desire in a man, and when you do, you'll begin to see those types of men begin showing up in your life.

Why You Need the List

In addition, the more you know about a man's likes and dislikes, the better equipped you are to relate to him well. For instance, if you know something about his hobbies, interests and desires, you can engage in conversation with him on those topics. If he likes home-cooked meals and you can cook, that will be valued by him. Also, when you later get to know his weaknesses, you can complement him in those areas and make him stronger. For example, if he lacks great social skills and you have an outgoing personality, you help him shine at corporate events and parties.

Sometimes we have to date men who we know are not our ideal mate to keep busy when other men frustrate us or act up. That's different than dating the wrong guy because we're desperate and scared that we won't find anybody new. This is strategically dating guys to keep our skills sharp and provide options until the right guy comes along. However, you may want to reserve your love, sex and intimacy to the highest bidder or the guy you value the most and think is best suited for you.

Note that it's important to not limit yourself when you're dating to just your ideal type. You need to have several options for dating so you won't be too pressed when the guy who matches your list comes along. Also, the goal is to get dates, so don't worry if he's not tall enough or wealthy enough. You need dates to start winning the dating game. You can't win if you don't practice and learn to compete. However, every guy you date is not going to end up your husband, or boyfriend for that matter. So I do recommend prioritizing your dates based upon your wish list.

Women can learn from men about dating. Men date all types of women, those they feel are "marriage potential" and those who are just "good for dating." They don't wait until they find "marriage potential" women before they go out on dates. They definitely know the difference between these types of women, but they don't let that stop them from enjoying dating both types. Woman will try to wait until they find that one guy who has "marriage potential" and then fixate on making the relationship work with him. This is often true even if that means they have to change the man to get him ready for marriage. In contrast, men don't waste time trying to change women; they have too much other important stuff to do. If he's interested in dating you, he will, and if he's not, he won't. If you don't meet his standard for "marriage potential," then you will just become "good for dating" until someone better comes along.

Women who fall into the "good for dating" category have to be careful not to be taken advantage of by the man. Men will use women who let them. This is not rocket science. However, I realized that men don't intentionally try to mislead us or string us along. He will simply see you as his "good enough for now chick" until better competition shows up. It's up to us to decide to get what we feel we want and deserve out of a relationship.

Action Item:

Answer the questions above for help in creating The List for your ideal mate based upon your needs, wants and desires. Determine your "Must Haves" and "Nice to Haves" on the list and use that to determine his value to you.

CHAPTER EIGHTEEN

Increase the Quantity and Quality of the Men You Meet

With today's competition, it's essential to become proactive about meeting men. I live in the DC Metro Area, and it is one of the most competitive areas to date. This is due to the male-to-female ratio, which happens to be one of the least advantageous to women in the country. In my county (Prince George's County, Maryland), there are only 76 men for every 100 single women.

You'll want to increase the quantity of men you date so that you can clearly determine which characteristics you want or need in a man. As you start dating and meeting more men, you will be able to better understand what characteristics and traits are important to you.

Some women have no problem meeting men; but for others, the good men are few and far between. This second group of women has a tendency to feel more pressed and act more desperate when they meet a man. This is why it's essential to increase the number of men you meet and date, even if they are not your ideal mate. It keeps you in practice 'til the right guy comes along.

Another reason to increase the quantity of men that you meet is to leverage the Rotation Strategy, which requires that you have no less than three men to date at any given time. The Rotation Strategy ensures that you have options to keep yourself busy so that you don't become too pressed or focused on only one guy. This is particularly important if you haven't dated in a while. It will be hard not to become focused or fixated on one guy because he's the only guy who has expressed any interest in you for some time. But until you are in a committed exclusive relationship, you should continue to have several guys as available date options.

If you meet a guy you like, don't get rid of the others and focus all of your energy and efforts on the one man you like. It's ok to have a prioritized order of the guys that you're dating, and as you meet new guys that you like more, you just remove the least favorite date from the rotation. If the guy at the top of the list doesn't call you, one of the others likely will. If guys feel they have competition, they sense it and will know that you are not pressed or desperate for them. It's helpful to begin to keep a calendar (online or a paper datebook) to ensure you can manage your dating schedule.

Having several men to date will build your confidence and self-esteem. It will allow you to hone your dating skills, such as improving your communication style on dates. We can date many men and enjoy their company until we find someone worth having a meaningful relationship with.

I would encourage you to learn to simply enjoy the company of men. Remember, I'm encouraging you to date, and not to have sex with many men. I'm not trying to encourage promiscuity. That is an individual choice that I personally do not advocate.

Best Ways to Meet Men

One thing I've learned is that men are approachable, even if they are in committed relationships. It's likely that approaching a guy will not be as hard as you think it is. Try approaching a guy and asking him a question (such as "What's a good place to get a cup of coffee?") or give him a compliment, and he will generally be polite, helpful and friendly—even if he's not interested. You will quickly tell if he has any interest in you or if he thinks you could be a cool friend to hang out with by the way he responds to you. If he shows no interest in you, thank him for the information and keep it moving. Practice approaching guys to increase your confidence.

Today there are so many ways to meet and date men. With online dating, personal matchmakers, speed dating and other methods, you should be able to increase the quantity of men you meet fairly quickly. In the past, women typically met men in grocery stores, gyms, bars/lounges, church, work, gyms/exercise centers, and car shows. These places are still great options for meeting men, but they have also gotten stale and simply don't generate the quantity of dates required for women to have enough options.

As an example, grocery stores will always be great places to meet men because everyone has to go and get food at some point. Guys are checking you out as well as your grocery cart, which helps them determine if you're single or in a committed relationship. Single servings of food are usually bought by single women. Alternatively, beer and men's toiletries in your basket means you're likely in a committed relationship. When you go to the grocery store and want to flirt, look casually cute and approachable and watch what you put into your basket.

Here are Some of the New, More Effective Ways to Meet Men:

Online Dating (Match.com, eHarmony)

Online dating has become a part of the mainstream for meeting prospective mates. Some online sites have posted a 400% sales growth each year. All types of people—attractive, busy professionals, Christians, creative types, etc.—all use this medium to meet new people. Online dating is much easier and cheaper than going out to bars and parties to meet people. It allows you to get to know the person before you actually meet them face-to-face. It helps you determine if it's worth spending your valuable time with them on a lunch or dinner date.

Online dating provides an opportunity to showcase your talents, gifts and, most important, your looks. You get to present yourself to the world, so be sure to put your best face forward. Your photo will be the most important part of your profile. Since this is true, be sure to get quality photos of you taken in several different outfits, and some of the photos should show some sexiness. Make sure you provide photos that present you well to men. I had several friends use an amateur photographer to take their photos for their online match profiles. Amateur photographers (see modelmayhem.com) will take your photos for a nominal cost or free to help build their portfolio and hone their skills. No matter how well you write your profile, you'll need to have an attractive, stand-out photo included in order to generate more responses. Profiles with no photos are hardly contacted.

Another key factor in online dating is writing your profile. Begin by viewing other profiles to get an idea of how a well-written profile is put together, and then tailor one to suit your interests and hobbies. Your dating profile has to begin with a headline, as it is the first thing members will read about you. It's worthwhile to put a little thought into your headline. Remember, the goal is to be an interesting person, even online, so take your time and put effort into your written profile.

There are many online dating sites that are available today. *Match.com* is one of the most popular sites, and it has over 15 million members. It's a great place to start due to the quantity of members, simplicity to use, and low monthly costs to join. *eHarmony*, which is also very popular, highlights their ability to do compatibility matching based upon your interests, characteristics and preferences for the type of mate you're seeking. eHarmony focuses on helping you achieve compatibility in the deep and meaningful ways that truly matter in a relationship.

What about some of the other online dating sites? Well, here's a sampling. *Greatboyfriends.com* allows a guy's ex-girlfriend or best female friend to describe him. This helps because it allows him to get a stamp of approval by other women, which carries more weight than anything he can say about himself. There is even an online site to help geeks meet, *gk2gk.com*. *Christiansingles.com* helps unattached Christian men and women meet one another. I offer an eBook on my website with 200+ online dating sites tailored to your own particular interests.

Speed Dating

Speed dating is for those who don't want to invest a lot of time in meeting new people, but they want to increase the quantity of people they meet. Speed dating provides four to five minute introductions of many men or women (about 20-25) at one event. It feels like a game, where a guy talks to a woman for four to five minutes, and then moves on to the next seat and talks to the next woman. The goal is to have a power introduction of yourself that lets you describe who you are in just a few short minutes. It is definitely fun. Instead of spending a lunch or dinner with someone who might be the wrong guy, you just spend four to five minutes with him. With a lot of people, this is enough time to determine if you want to see them again. In speed dating, you meet a lot of men in a short time-frame. At the end of the evening, contact info is exchanged between the men and women who are both interested in each other.

Upscale Single Nights

These are upscale events planned for busy professionals based upon similar interests, such as hiking, sports, salsa dancing, and gourmet cooking. Most larger cities offer these types of gatherings, and they are a win-win scenario. Even if you don't meet a new guy, you'll have fun because there is a focus on your hobbies and interests.

Personal Matchmaking Services
(Master Matchmakers, Selective Search, It's Just Lunch)

Personal matchmaking services have gotten more popular in the last few years. These services work for you because you pay them to find a match. Most of these services conduct a phone or in-person interview covering your background and preferences in a mate. Your assigned matchmaker researches and screens matches for you until a suitable mate is found. If both individuals accept the match, an introduction between the two is arranged so they can meet and schedule a date. Most good matchmaking services cost at least $1,000 because of all the work to search and find someone suitable for you. There are also some very high end matchmakers that charge $10,000 or more due to their ability to match you with upscale, wealthy individuals. Some of the personal matchmaking services that I have personally used or know others who have personally used are *Master Matchmakers, Selective Search*, and *It's Just Lunch*.

Master Matchmakers and Selective Search are high-end matchmaking services; they're designed to provide educated, cultured, successful men and women, with a strong desire for a committed relationship, with an opportunity to meet potential mates. These services will interview you and really work to know your specific needs, wants and desires; their focus is on finding a suitable match for you.

It's Just Lunch is a matchmaking service for those looking for a stress-free way to meet other singles without all the pressure that typical dating can bring. The arranged dates are short, sweet, and never over dinner, typically over lunch or after dinner drinks.

Unique Ideas for Meeting Men

- *Networking House Parties* based upon specific topic areas, such as learning to ski or staring a new business (This will generate people with like interests.)

- ***Monday Night Football Parties,*** which will always bring out many men.

- ***Find a Date for a Friend:*** If you have a close single friend who knows you well, have her find a date for you and you find a date for her. Her search for you can be done at work, parties or the grocery store. The goal is that each of you will be on the lookout for a guy for the other one. Enlisting friends to help you find a mate is never a bad idea.

- ***Multi-Level Networking Happy Hours:*** Five women each invite three males that they know and five guys each invite three women, and soon you'll have a party with good quality men and women who are all looking to meet new people. You could continue where the invitees then invite three people they know, which just creates a larger party.

Meeting Specific Types of Men

If you know the type of man you're interested in, then you could pinpoint locations based upon the type of mate you're looking for. The goal is to choose the best locations to meet the type of men that meet your specific wants, desires and needs.

Meeting Men of Faith

If you are interested in meeting men who are putting in effort to grow spiritually, then attend church and join their singles ministry. The singles ministry at most churches provide wholesome ways to meet and mingle with singles who are looking to strengthen their faith and grow spiritually. Also, if you attend the 8 a.m. or early service of most churches, you tend to get the really committed guys. Attending worship service at 8 a.m. means he probably wasn't out partying the night before and he is eager to attend church.

Meeting Blue Collar Men

I have met a ton of blue collar men in construction stores such as Home Depot and Lowe's, which are both great places to meet them. Sometimes I just go to those stores to flirt just because I love men. If you approach men with questions about how to fix something in your home, they will be more than happy to guide you in the right direction. You could also just walk past any construction site as the workers never seem to hesitate to speak to attractive women walking by.

Meeting Professional Men

If you don't want to date men at your current job, then attend industry events to network and meet new men. For instance, each industry has associations that gather regularly to advance knowledge sharing in a particular field. I've found that the annual conference of the National MBA Association is an awesome place to meet professional men. For social events, ski networking parties and corporate golf tournaments are great places to mingle with new men. One of my favorite places to come across professional men is in menswear stores (like Thomas Pink, Barney's or Brooks Brothers). Men are there to obviously buy suits, ties and shoes for their corporate jobs, and they could use some advice from women as they try on things. Always be looking to purchase something for a male you know, otherwise you could seem like a stalker hanging out in the menswear store with no man with you. Other places to meet professional men include golf stores.

Meeting Good-Time Guys

Good time, party guys can be found in nightclubs. Personally, I think clubs are one of the more challenging places to meet a man. In general, the clubs are dark, loud, and full of drunk people. Most people, including men, go to clubs in groups. Ladies even go to the bathroom at least in pairs. There are very few opportunities to meet and get to know someone in a club. In fact, it's hard to truly see what someone looks like in a club. If you'd like to meet guys in the club, be open-minded and not so guarded, and by all means, dance and enjoy yourself.

Meeting Rich Men

I know some women who are doing really well professionally and financially, and they want a guy who is doing as well or better than them. However, I would encourage all women to not judge men solely based upon the kind of work they do. There are some great quality men who don't earn a lot of money but are honest, fun, and God-fearing, and they know how to treat a woman well. However, if your mind is made up and you want a rich man, here are few facts that you need to know:

- There is not a large availability of rich millionaires. Statistics show that there are only about 100,000 men in the US who earn an income in excess of $1 million a year and have a net worth of over $10 million dollars. Over half of them live in New York City (Manhattan), Palm Beach, Los Angeles and Aspen. Keep in mind that there over 17 million single women (in the 20-45 age range). If you do the math, that is a very small number of rich men to single woman.

- Rich men can have their pick of beautiful, sexy and attractive women. These men are looking for the queen of queens, someone who can add glamour and beauty to his already impressive life. She not only should be beautiful outside, but also smart, talented and damn near perfect. His expectations are really high.

Rich men are a special type of man, and they come with their own share of challenges. Some are athletes or entertainers. The majority of the ones that I have met are in business, and there are some wildly successful men in Corporate America and on Wall Street. When I was a Vice President at a Fortune 500 company, I had the opportunity to be exposed to many of these successful, wealthy men. They are generally smart, educated, polished and financially astute. However, they don't have much time for anything but their career.

Assuming you have decided to pursue rich men, you have to put yourself in the right place at the right time to gain access to them. As an example, there are certain neighborhoods in all cities where old money people typically live. In my area, Annapolis, Maryland is one area, as well as Potomac, Maryland and Tysons/Great Falls in Northern Virginia. You could hang out in those neighborhoods, by going to the grocery store or coffee shop or even taking golf or tennis lessons there; that way, you put yourself in a position to meet rich men. Socializing with the rich doesn't have to cost a significant amount of money. Some other places to meet rich men include:

- Volunteering for charity and political fundraisers – Some of these events are thousands of dollars for the ticket, but the after parties are generally a lot cheaper. As an example, I went to the Congressional Black Caucus after party for $75, because the gala dinner ticket was $750 per seat. Of course, if you volunteer, the event will likely be free.

- Taking lessons for certain types of social sports which rich men participate in: sailing, golf, tennis and horseback riding

- Attending equestrian events such as polo or races like the Kentucky Derby

- Going to auctions

- Learning to fly

- Cigar bars (Successful men tend to frequent cigar bars, and if you don't mind the smoke, it's a great place to meet them.)

- Checking out pet shows (There are rare breed dogs that make expensive pets.)

- Traveling to exclusive resorts

- VIP lounges in airports (Women who look like they belong with a rich man can walk into a VIP airport lounge with confidence, and she will rarely be asked to leave.)

- Buying season tickets to sporting events, especially to club level access

- Crashing parties, galas and events (There are even books about how to successfully crash parties.)

You can also take part-time jobs to meet the rich. A few ideas are:

- ✴ Hostessing at an exclusive private club or restaurant

- ✴ Working at a fine art gallery

- ✴ Finding employment at an exclusive resort

- ✴ Becoming a concierge at an expensive hotel

- ✴ Getting a job as a flight attendant for private jets

You also have to watch for those men who are pretending to be wealthier than they actually are. External signs of wealth don't always tell you the magnitude and quality of a man's fortune. A man with new money generally has a look that shows it off. I mean their suits, clothing, home, type of watch; they all will indicate that he has money. However, a man with old money will wear a more traditional style of clothes that he's worn his entire life, and his attire will be very understated.

There are numerous books on meeting rich millionaires (e.g., *How to Meet the Rich: For Business, Friendship or Romance* by Ginie Sayles) if you are genuinely interested in pursuing these men. Some books go so far as to tell you what specific places/events to attend to meet rich men in each city. My basic advice is to be deliberate about putting yourself in a position to meet rich men, if that is who you are looking for.

Don't Let Girlfriends Minimize Your Ability to Meet Men

Most women have a more attractive or drop-dead gorgeous girlfriend that they hang out with. This situation can be overcome in several ways so that you can get your fair share of attention. First, having a gorgeous friend is good because she can get you into VIP rooms and open up other opportunities to meet more guys. One thing to remember is that there are a lot of men who know they don't stand a chance with her, so they will go to the woman they feel is more approachable, which may be you. The other thing to do is to hang out with friends who have a different look or style than you; that way, you'll each attract different types of men. One of my girlfriends is earthy and Afrocentric, with natural hair; she attracts guys that I generally do not.

Let's say you're looking to meet men and you have a girlfriend who is a cockblocker. You know, this is the type of woman who says something negative about every guy who wants to talk to you. Be sure to separate yourself from her so guys stand a chance of talking to you. Mingle alone and meet up with your girlfriend at pre-arranged timeframes. Sometimes a girlfriend can simply be too clingy. When I go out, I like to meet men. Remember the title is why I love men. So, clingy girlfriends don't give me a time to mingle and enjoy male companionship. So, mingle alone and meet up with your girlfriend at pre-arranged timeframes.

Action Item:

Determine which methods and places you will leverage to meet new men. Ensure you choose several methods and places so that you increase the quantity of men you meet.

CHAPTER NINETEEN

Know Where and How to Date Him

How many people enjoy first dates? The first date is one of the most important events in a new relationship. First dates are important because they can either make a man eager to see you again or make him run for the highway. Know that chivalry is not dead. Expect a man to ask for and take you out on a first date. But be sure to drive your own car to the location in case the date goes horribly bad and you need to leave as quickly as possible.

Let me back up for one second. Let's say you meet a guy, and for the first date, he asks to come to your place or wants you to cook dinner for him (at your place). I'd say that most likely he is married, in a relationship, or trying to make you his jump-off. If you let a man come to your house and that is the first date, you decide if that's the type of relationship you want before you get involved with him.

One of the most important things to consider on a first date is the location. That's because the location will affect the way you interact with each other; the goal should be to find an environment where you'll both feel relaxed and comfortable.

Good First Date Locations

Here are the types of locations that work best for a first date:

* **Bowling/Playing Pool:** This can be fun, and it's a great way to flirt. With pool, you get to wear your sexy jeans and lean over the pool table suggestively.

* **Golfing/Miniature Golfing:** Both golf and putt-putt are great options for enjoying the weather and scenery and spending quality time talking. If you're on a regular golf course, you may want to only play 9 holes, as an 18-hole round could take about four hours. If the date is not going well, that could be way too much time to be together.

* **Lunch/Brunch:** This type of meal allows for good conversation, and it's also quick. Plus the date won't take the prime time of the day if it doesn't work out.

* **Dinner:** This is good if you've had a few conversations by phone and know that you can tolerate him through an entire dinner. A nice quiet restaurant can be a great place to converse and continue to get to know each other.

Bad First Date Locations:

Here are the types of locations that are not good for a first date:

* **Movies:** The room is dark, and you don't get to see or talk to your date.

* **Music Concerts:** The music is loud, and there's always something more interesting for him to see, such as the artist who is performing.

* **Visiting a Park:** I wouldn't suggest spending time

in a remote place like a park, as it is unsafe unless you're certain that he is not a serial killer.

* **Your Home:** If he asks to come over to your house on the first date, then you will likely not get any dates outside the house. His primary purpose is probably to have sex with you, not court or date you.

What to Talk about on the First Date

The goals of communication between a man and a woman are fundamentally different. Women use communication to bond socially or romantically with the person they are conversing with. Men tend to communicate to exchange information or solve a problem. A woman will communicate simply because she enjoys talking, whereas the man is usually more interested in trading information.

When it comes to communicating, it is important to create some mystery and intrigue about you. A woman is sometimes too eager to tell a man everything about herself. Don't overcommunicate with a man on a first date by telling him too much information about yourself. Leave some mystery and allure; allow him to get to know more and more about you over time. He should want to know more about you each time he sees you, not run because you've told him way too much already.

Another key factor about communicating with a man is to display intelligence. If a man is successful, he expects his woman to be intelligent because our partners in life are a reflection of who we are and what we want out of life. It makes a man look better to family, friends and co-workers if you are intelligent. That way, you'll be able to easily converse at company events and family gatherings. People will be impressed because his woman is beautiful and intelligent. Remember beauty is what gets his attention, but intelligence is one of the ways to keep him.

Additionally, men like women who communicate clearly and succinctly. Listen to the way that men communicate to one another. Avoid mushy, emotional conversation as much as possible. He is not interested in talking about your feelings on a first date, keep it light and fun. Suggestions for topics to talk about on your first date include:

- His interests or hobbies
- Sports
- Interesting books or magazines (*People* magazine does not count.)
- Movies, plays or theater
- His work/job
- Your work/job
- Current news or pop culture topics

What Not to Talk about on a First Date

Let a guy get to know you before you begin to share too many details about your views and your past. For most of us, the rough times in our lives have allowed us to grow and become the people we are today. However, until someone gets to know you, they may not understand or may pass judgments on some your past mistakes. Here are some tips for what NOT to talk about on your first date:

❧ **Getting Married:** It scares men to get married to someone they love. This is definitely not a conversation he wants to have with a woman he barely knows.

❧ **Your Kids:** You love your kids and they interest you. However, to a man, this just indicates increased responsibility or baby daddy drama.

❧ **Your Horrible Childhood:** Don't seek pity for injustices in your past; it will make you appear hurt, wounded and in need of healing.

❧ **Ex-Boyfriends:** This is a no-win situation. If you say something positive about an ex-boyfriend, a man will feel threatened or discouraged. If you say how he cheated on you constantly, he will think you are weak and a pushover. The truth is that there's no good outcome likely to result from talking about an ex on the first date. I remember a guy once asked about one of my past boyfriends, and I talked about him for about 20 minutes. My date then said: "Enough about your ex!" I replied, "Well, you asked and there's so many great things to share. We could be talking about him all night." Needless to say, that didn't go over well. My point is that the purpose of the date is to get to know each other, and the conversation should be about you and him.

❧ **Politics:** I am passionate about my politics. Nobody better say anything bad about Obama! Just kidding! People are generally passionate about their political beliefs, and these conversations can wait until later.

- **Death or Depressing Events:** Do I even need to explain why you shouldn't talk about death or depressing news?

- **Sex:** If you start a conversation about sex, the guy will take it over and won't be able to focus on any other topic for the rest of the night. There needs to be some things that are mysterious about you. Talking details about sex takes some of the intrigue and mystique away from the actual sexual encounter.

- **Therapy or Rehab:** He doesn't need to know how well your therapy or rehab sessions are going. He also doesn't need to know that you had a nervous breakdown (if you did), at least not on the first date.

If a guy is interested in a second date, he will likely try to make plans for it before you end the first one. Or an interested man will contact you within a few days to try and schedule another date to see you. If he calls you a few weeks after your date, he's really not that interested in you. You may be "good for dating" until someone better comes along; however, know that his interest is low or he wouldn't wait that long to contact you. Additionally, he probably doesn't really care whether or not you say yes or no, it's just something for him to do. If, at the end of the date, he says, "I'll call you," he might; still, oftentimes that's a filler because he doesn't want to say he's no longer interested. If you call him once, and he doesn't return your call, try him again in about a week. If you haven't heard from him after calling once or twice, just stop calling. He's moved on. Other reasons that a man doesn't call or make plans right away include having some drama/crisis going on in his life or emotional hang-ups. This means no follow-through can be a sign of low interest or a red flag.

Having Sex on the First Date

A man still holds a woman to a higher sexual standard than he holds for himself. Most men don't want to think of their wife as promiscuous or easy. In fact, if he could delete all of her prior sexual experiences, he would. After you sleep with a man, the balance of power starts to shift in his favor. By sleeping with him on the first date, you could end the need for him to court or pursue you, and his primary interest in you could just be for sex.

Women generally don't like to have sex on the first date, because we really don't like being a victim of a "hit-and-run." However, in this day and age, if you decide to have sex on the first date, it should be your own decision based upon want you want. You should already know that there is a good chance that he may not call you anymore, but that's the chance you take. Men rarely turn down sex, and they don't need to be in love or in a relationship with you to have sex. There are many women who feel that way about sex nowadays, too.

Having sex on the first date can sometimes depend on the circumstances. Let's say you have a date with a guy, and it ends up lasting all day because you really hit it off quickly. Then "things" just happen. In that case, there's a good chance he may want to continue seeing you. However, if you met him a club, and then had sex at about 4 a.m. at your place, there's a very good chance you will not hear from him again. If you're looking to just have fun with him, enjoy yourself. If you see him having some serious love potential, then it may make sense to wait. It is generally best to wait to have sex if you want him to consider you a serious long-term partner.

I have learned that men will be pretty honest about your sexual encounter if you ask them, outside the bedroom, of course. If you have sex with a guy, don't make assumptions.

- Having sex with him doesn't mean he will continue to call you or ever call you again.

- Having sex with him doesn't mean he won't be having sex with other women.

- Having sex with him doesn't mean that you're entering a committed relationship with him.

- Having sex with him doesn't mean that getting to know you better will be a primary focus in his life.

If you find yourself in situations where you often have sex too soon, then we'll assume holding out is not your strong suit. An easy suggestion for overcoming this is to not be physically ready to have sex when you go out on a date. This could include not shaving your legs or underarms, wearing big granny panties, or wearing clothes that are difficult to get out of. If you really don't want to have sex with him, but you don't trust yourself, then some of these tactics may work for you.

Based on every man that I know, I can tell you that having sex is very important to them. It might even be at the top of the list of their favorite things to do. You have to remember that men can have sex with a total stranger and find it physically enjoyable. Meanwhile, even though some women have gotten comfortable with having sex on the first date, they still are more likely to want and desire love from that person more than men. Women do want the physical enjoyment of sex, but they also desire the love and intimacy that comes through lovemaking. Sometimes we want love so bad, we confuse lovemaking with sex, but they are two different things. Lovemaking starts while you're on your feet, when you love and care for a person. However, sex is the easy part, as it is a physical act for pleasure and enjoyment. Most people would agree that sex is even more fulfilling when it is accompanied by lovemaking, when deep feelings exist between the two people.

Action Item:

Think about all the first dates that you've had and consider the location. Did your relationship get off on the wrong foot because you didn't start things out properly on the first date?

CHAPTER TWENTY

Check Him Out

take the position that most people have skeletons in their closet. The question is how many bones are in the closet and is the dead body still attached to those bones? Everyone has something they keep quiet; those things they would be too embarrassed or ashamed to tell anyone. But then there are those deep dark secrets that it's best to dis-

Innocent Questions	What the Answers Tell You
What sports did you play in high school?	This will allow him to discuss how athletic or fit he is or how he views fitness in general.
Where do you spend time for the holidays? Does your mom live nearby?	This helps you understand how close he is to his family. If he doesn't have a relationship with his mother, and she is living, I'm always a bit concerned.
Are you an only child? Do you have any nieces or nephews?	This allows him to open up about his childhood, or how he feels about children in general.

Innocent Questions	What the Answers Tell You
If you didn't have to go to work, how would you spend your day?	This helps you understand what other interests or passions he has in life. It may also reveal his attitudes about work.
What did you do in your last job?	Usually, he will open up about his current job to contrast it with his last job.
Have you ever been to Las Vegas or Atlantic City?	This tells you how he views gambling. For me, if he says he hates gambling, then we can end the date right then. Just kidding!
Did you like school? What was your favorite class?	This helps you understand if he likes studying and learning over-all. One of my favorite hobbies is reading, so if he never reads or doesn't like to learn anything new that would be a challenge for me. My mom always said, "If I only had money to buy a book or a meal, I would choose the book."
What's your favorite drink?	This helps you understand if he's a heavy drinker, casual drinker, or doesn't drink at all.

cover early. That way, you can make an informed decision about whether or not you want to get involved with a guy.

I assume that men operate on a "need-to-know" basis in terms of what they reveal. If you don't specifically ask, then assume he won't volunteer information. I was dating a guy who seemed to only call during the day, from work or while in his car, which is generally a sign that he cannot call you from his house. I remember asking him if he lived with any "crazy girlfriends" and he said no. When I later found out that he lived with his girlfriend, I said, "I thought you said you didn't live with a girlfriend." He replied, "You asked if I lived with any 'crazy girlfriends' and I said no, because she's not crazy. She's actually very cool." I learned the hard way that day that we need to be as specific as possible to get a better sense of who he is and if he's trustworthy.

It's important to check men out and be safe about dating and mating. Some men (and women) are crazy. If you've ever had a stalker, you would know how serious it is to be safe and protect yourself from dangerous and mentally unstable people. When I was in college, I had a stalker who would send flowers to my apartment, and take photos of me while I was sitting in class and then mail them to me. He obviously knew where I lived. However, I didn't know who was doing this. When I was in class, and he took my picture, he was around me at times and I never even knew it. To this day, I've never figured out who he was. Ever since that experience, I have been extremely wary of men.

You need to know about his upbringing and the people in his close circle. Did his mother raise him or was he adopted? Did he have a stable or unstable childhood?

What is his religious background? What are his beliefs and convictions? Has he been married before, and if so, why did it end? Does he have children? Does he support and spend time with his children? Are all of his friends divorced? And my favorite, you need to know about his sexual health. For me, this is so important; I have always been adamant about maintaining perfect sexual health. My OBGYN thinks I'm paranoid because I am so serious about protecting myself from diseases and illnesses. But my attitude is that sexual health is extremely important for women. There are many STDs, and if left untreated, even just one of them could cause damage to your reproductive organs, potentially resulting in sterility or even death.

Now before you solicit an FBI agent to conduct a background check on him, you can start by asking simple, basic questions and really listen to the man's answers. I don't mean to quiz him to death by asking a bunch of heavy questions when you first meet him, but ask little innocent questions that will begin to draw out clues about who he is. If you ask him if it's ok for you to chew gum in his car (a very innocent question), his response will tell you how he values his materialistic possessions. I use this example because I once asked a guy this question, and he emphatically told me, "No food or eating allowed in my car, including gum." I thought to myself, This guy is really anal, and we may have some challenges. Meanwhile, I was remembering the time that I ate BBQ ribs and cole slaw all while sitting in my car as I waited for my friend to finish shopping.

Here are examples of some of the innocent questions that will help you better understand him:

Once you begin to better understand who he is by asking innocent questions, you could continue to check him out further by leveraging today's online tools to conduct further investigation. You can do online background checks (for criminal offenses) or simply just google his name, and narrow down the search by adding his city and state. If you have the cash, and you think he's important to your future, you might hire a private detective to check him out. I have personally never hired a private detective to check out a guy. If I felt I even needed to hire one, that already means I have some serious concerns about his background. I would rather rely on my intuition to determine if it makes sense to continue to get to know him.

Sometimes there are cheaper ways to personally check a man out and better understand him. One way is to go to his job. Now, of course, I do not mean to show up at his job by surprise or without an invitation; if you do, you will be perceived as a little crazy. Instead, you could ask him if you can come by and take him to lunch one day or meet him at his job after work to go to a sporting event together (some place where it wouldn't make sense to drive two separate cars). One of my girlfriends dated a guy for a year who said he worked as a teacher, only to find out that he had no job the entire time they dated. I guess that's why he always wanted to come to her place, opposed to going out for dinner.

Before you get too serious with a guy, be sure you have asked him some innocent questions to get to know who he is and how he lives his life. Innocent questions can lead to big clues for major personality or character flaws.

Action Item:

Conduct an online background check on yourself so you can get a feeling for the type of information that can be provided through the reports. This will also help you get comfortable with the process in case you ever need to conduct a background check on a guy you're dating.

CHAPTER TWENTY ONE

Learn to Stroke His Ego

We must learn to stroke and befriend a man's ego. We have to be very careful of possibly bruising his ego. The male ego is very fragile, and it needs to be handled with care. Be sure to praise and compliment his efforts. If you stroke his ego, it will put your man in a position of power, and he will want and feel the need to protect and take care of you.

Men like to please women. In turn, you'll want to appreciate him and show him that he pleases you. Let him know when he makes you happy. If he feels that he cannot please you or meet your needs, his ego won't allow him to stay. If a woman is never satisfied or she's unrealistically demanding, he may come to realize that he can never please her and simply get tired of trying. Men would rather be alone than to be with a woman who makes him feel inadequate or disrespected. Men like and need to be admired and respected, especially by their woman. If you express interest in his views and opinions, you are showing that you value his intelligence and trust his judgment. If you look up to him and he is your hero, let him know.

Be sincere in your praise and compliments. Do not be insincere; if you are still with him, there should be something you can find to compliment him on. I know you can find at least one thing that is special about him, even if it's how funny, witty, smart or stylish he is. I remember dating a guy and the best thing about him was his biceps. I'm sure there had to be other great characteristics, but the main thing that I recognized was those biceps. I never hesitated to tell him how great his biceps looked; they were picture perfect and really something special.

You could also appreciate him for fixing things around the house. Men are problem-solvers and need to be appreciated for their fixing, repairing and rebuilding abilities. Also, respect his knowledge, talents, opinions and decisions. You do this by not debating or arguing with him on every decision he makes; it's important to trust his judgment.

And by all means, do not disrespect him in public or even tease or belittle him in public. Find every opportunity to demonstrate how much you appreciate him through your words and actions. Let him know you trust him, respect him, and are proud of him. If you really do, you shouldn't hesitate to tell him. A man can even perform better on his job if he has a woman at home who supports and believes in him; it will spill over into his confidence at work as well as home. When he is affirmed by you, a man feels that he can conquer the world.

Avoid Ego-Busters

There are certain aspects of a man that he can be sensitive about; criticizing him can bruise his ego or hurt him deeply. It's important to avoid these ego-busters, as they are tough for him to recover from.

Penis Size:

I would stay away from making comments or jokes about his penis, unless you have something you're certain will be reassuring and perceived as genuine. If men are making jokes at each other's expense, they often make fun of penis size or performance issues. If a woman makes jokes about a man's penis size, it really bruises his ego.

Hair:

Men can be very sensitive about thinning hair or going bald, or even turning gray. It means they're getting older and losing their sexual prowess. However, a completely bald man (not the partially bald look that George Jefferson had on the TV show, The Jeffersons) is very sexy, so be sure to let him know. It will make him feel better about his look. If a man is turning gray, let him know that gray hair is a sign of maturity and wisdom.

Money:

Success and money are sexy. Having money generally makes a less attractive man very attractive and appealing. Men know that having money is attractive to women, and the more they have, the more women they attract. If a man has no or little money, he could be sensitive about it and about not being where he wants to be financially. Don't make him feel bad if he is working hard to improve his financial status in life.

Height:

Most men who are not very tall are insecure about it. Don't make him feel bad by constantly commenting on it.

Action Item:

List three specific things that you like or respect about the guy you are dating. Next, begin to share those things with him when it is most appropriate. Be sincere and genuine in your compliments and praise, and your man will appreciate you for it!

PART IV
THE TRUTHS AND LESSONS LEARNED FROM DATING

THE TRUTHS AND LESSONS
LEARNED FROM DATING

In this section, I share the lessons learned and truths about men, love, dating and relationships. I will help you understand more about how men think, based upon what they have told me, as I have spent my entire life being around men. I'll reveal insights into the minds of men and uncover the secrets for attracting and keeping the men you want in your life. I had to learn these lessons the hard way, but I am now smarter and finally winning the dating game.

Some of what I learned about men, love, dating and relationships may be hard to accept; however, in my experience, I have found all of this to be true. Stay aware that the information in Part IV is intended to enlighten you, not discourage you. Be open-minded and use this information to gain a better perspective on love and relationships.

CHAPTER TWENTY TWO

The Truth about Men

Men Cheat on Women They Love

believe that men are not naturally monogamous. In fact, I think monogamy is unnatural for men. Men like sexual variety. A man's natural tendency is to want and desire new sexual partners. As one comedian said, the only thing men like better than "bleep" is new "bleep." Men will lust after other women even when they're perfectly happy and fulfilled in a relationship with the woman they love. I do not condone cheating, but I do realize that cheating does not necessarily indicate any dissatisfaction in his relationship with you. That's why we wonder why a man can cheat on a beautiful woman with a less attractive woman. But for the man, it's just about variety and wanting something different.

I believe that a man can make a spiritual commitment to one woman and be monogamous and committed to her. However, even when men marry and make a vow of loyalty and faithfulness ("until death do us part"), they may cheat anyway. The primary thing that stops them from cheating is fear of losing the woman they love or no real good opportunities to cheat have arisen. However, if they were sure they could get away with it and their wife or girlfriend would never know, most men would have sex with other women. In those periods during a relationship when a man is monogamous, he still may satisfy his need for variety through porn and strip club hopping.

Many men think about other women all the time but it may have no reflection on how attractive he finds you. Men often cheat because they lack self-control or the discipline to resist sex with someone different. So, as a woman, don't take this too personally. It's not about anything you did or didn't do; it's just men's natural desire for the variety that new sexual partners provide. Women often have sex for an emotional connection and men can too. But many times with men, it is not about intimacy or love; sex is just about sex.

One of my friends told me that after you get married, there is no more sex. The reality is that your man may be still getting sex; he's just grown tired or bored with having sex with you. Now I'm not saying it's impossible for a man to remain monogamous for his entire relationship, because I'm sure there are one or two guys out there who are monogamous. I've just never met many of them.

Men Really Don't Want to Be Changed

Men rarely change so it's important to evaluate a man based on who he is right now. It's like buying shoes from the clearance rack when they say "sold as is." Whatever nicks or flaws they have are the "as is," so take 'em or leave 'em. Take a long hard look at who he is now and see if he's a good fit for you today. Don't bank on a lot on major changes to occur. Not that he can't or won't change. People transform their lives all the time. There is nothing wrong with encouraging and supporting him if he is seeking to change or improve some areas in his life. However, it is not your responsibility to change him. If he wants to change, he will, but on his own and in his own time. So, know that men don't want to be changed by you. Enjoy him for who he is or leave him alone.

It is perfectly fine to clearly communicate what you expect and need from your man, and always be straightforward in your communication with him. However, don't try to change him into something he's not. You have a right to tell a man what you don't like about the way he makes you feel, and how he responds to your comments will determine if he's interested in changing his behavior for you. If he doesn't change for you, don't blame him. You are responsible for your feelings. When a relationship doesn't work out, it doesn't always mean someone is inadequate; it just means that you're not a good fit for each other. Why hold onto something that is not working? Sometimes we try to hang onto relationships that God wants us to get out of so he can bring something better into our life.

Men don't waste time trying to change women; they have lots of other important stuff to do. If he's interested in dating you, he will, and if he's not, he won't. If you don't meet his standard for "marriage potential," then you will just become "good for dating" until someone better comes along. A man accepts you for who you are.

I am not saying compromise on your wants and needs in a relationship, but I am saying that you have to accept him for who he is. One of the most endearing things you can do for a man is to accept and approve of him. Have a basic understanding and acceptance of who he is, add in hot meals and regular sex, and you'll be on your way to a man's heart!

Don't Underestimate the Relationship Between a Man and His Mother

One of the most important introductions that you will have is when you meet a man's mother. If a man wants you to meet his mother or family, this means he's getting serious about you. When that opportunity comes, be ready for it, and take the introduction quite seriously. I have three brothers and if Mom doesn't like one of my brother's girlfriends, she doesn't hesitate to let them know.

A wise woman understands the precious bond between a man and his mother. You're not going to change it nor would you want to. A mother is very proud of her son, especially if he's a good man. He will want to take care of his mother and make sure that she has what she needs in life, especially as his mother gets older. His mother values him. You will have to prove your worth to his mother as she is protective of him and wants only the best for her son. When I got married, my mother-in-law loved me for her son. We got along great and she thought we were so perfect together. Still, I knew my role and knew she didn't play around when it came to what is best for her son.

A huge red flag for me is when a guy doesn't have any relationship with his mother, and she is still living. Or if he speaks to his mother in a disrespectful or harsh manner, he will likely treat you the same way.

Competing with a man's mother is a lose-lose situation. You will not win. His mom has loved him unconditionally all his life, and well, you, not so long. If you want a smooth relationship with your man, establishing or improving your relationship with his mother is key.

If you were to get married to him, your marriage to him will not just be you and him; you are also combining two families who will need to get along to keep things smooth and healthy. It is also in your best interest to keep things smooth and polite with his ex-wife or baby's mama, as most men don't want unnecessary drama in their homes. They want their home to be a place of peace.

Cooking Is Still Important to Modern Men

It's important to understand the psychology of cooking for men. There is something inherently nurturing and loving about cooking for your man. First, it takes time to go shopping for the foods, to prepare and cut up the vegetables, etc., and then cook the food. Cooking a special meal can easily take a few hours. I like watching the anticipation on a guy's face as he waits for the succulent, mouth-watering meal. Cooking also provides the opportunity for you to spend quality time talking over dinner, and enjoying good conversation with your man since he's feeling relaxed.

Have you ever asked a guy what his favorite food is that his mom used to cook for him? He can name it immediately. My ex-husband always talked about his mama's bread pudding. Whenever we went to a restaurant, he would order bread pudding, and after eating it, he'd say, "It's good, but not like Mama's." One of the reasons men grow so attached to their mom is because of the way she fed him over the years. If a man meets a beautiful woman who can also cook, he thinks he's found a treasure or gold mine.

I will admit that with the majority of the men I date, I do not cook for them. However, if I do cook for a man, I know that I really like him and want to impress him. I grew up in a family with a grandmother and aunts who could really cook great soul food. Although my cooking doesn't compare to theirs, I do have my specialty items that would rate up there with the top chefs in the country. Every woman should have at least two or three meals that she can prepare really well so that she can treat her man to a home-cooked meal or simply enjoy it herself.

Kissing Tells You a Lot about His Feelings for You

When a man and woman lock lips and kiss for the first time, if it's right, it ignites sparks and magic. To a guy, kissing is a more intimate act than having sex. So kissing is a good guide to tell you how he feels about you. Here are some guidelines that will help you understand how he feels about you based upon how he kisses you:

- If he kisses you deep and long, he's interested in getting to know you better.
- If he kisses you and makes eye contact for a long time, he just might be falling in love with you.
- If he kisses you on your forehead or face, he absolutely adores you.
- If he kisses your booty, he simply loves your booty (and you too).
- If he doesn't kiss you at all and still has sex with you, he's not really interested in you. He likely just wants to have sex with you.

CHAPTER TWENTY THREE

The Truth About Love and Relationships

Romantic Love Is the Number One Ilusion for Single Women

Many women dream of meeting "the one," getting married, and living happily ever after. As women, we all dream of romance and falling in love with that special person. This type of love is known as *Eros love*, which is that emotional or romantic love that constitutes the feeling of being "in love." Eros love is that intense sexual desire or overwhelming longing or craving for someone.

However, there are other types of love that we need in our life, namely *Philos love* (friendship love) and *Agape love* (unconditional love). Philos love is about companionship and connecting with people to share life's journey. Philos love is based on friendship, and friendship is the foundation of successful relationships. Agape love is unconditional love and it is from God. Agape love is above Philos love and Eros love. It is a love that is totally selfless, when a person gives love to another person even if this act does not benefit her/him in any way.

To feel completely satisfied and fulfilled, we need all three loves to be present in our lives. However, too many women only focus on romantic (Eros) love, and they look for a man to "complete" them. They just want to get married and "live happily ever after."

I don't believe that I have to be married and have a husband to be complete and happy. I know that if my life isn't already fulfilled when I meet a man, than neither he nor marriage can make me happy or fulfilled. Nothing outside of you can produce long-lasting satisfaction and happiness—no man, money, job, house or car can produce true fulfillment in life. I personally have only been able to maintain peace in my life through a relationship with God. Find balance in your love relationships, not by focusing just on a romantic (Eros) love, but also by creating Philos and Agape love relationships in your life.

Relationships Are Opportunities for Spiritual Growth

What if I were to tell you that relationships are opportunities to discover your capacity to love, forgive, heal and grow as a person. Since relationships spark the best and worst in us, they provide an opportunity for growth and spiritual development. Relationships allow mutual expression and sharing between two people, which makes it the ultimate tool for self-assessment and personal development.

Some of us think a relationship's primary purpose is to fulfill our needs and desires. We begin to think of relationships in terms of what we can get from someone. Some of us are waiting for a romantic relationship to end boredom, loneliness, depression or insecurity.

I think of relationships as our assignments in life. We

are assigned people from whom we can learn valuable lessons. That's why we have to focus on learning and growing from our experience with our romantic partners—not on making them "the one." When a person leaves our life, it may be because the lesson has been learned; so learn the lesson, use it to help yourself grow, and be optimistic about what life has to offer you next.

God brings people into our life that provide the maximal opportunity for mutual growth. If you've been repeating the same type of experiences with men, it may be that you have yet to learn the lessons that will allow you to grow from those relationships. Ask yourself, "Am I learning from my relationships? If so, what am I learning?"

Relationships provide several levels of teaching and learning. The first level of teaching comes from what is known as the *casual encounter*, such as people we meet in an elevator or at the grocery store. At this level, these casual encounters allow us to refine our personalities. Our personal weaknesses that are evident in casual encounters typically appear magnified in more intimate relationships. If we are rude and nasty with the grocery store clerk, we will likely be rude and nasty with the individuals we love the most.

The second level of teaching is *a more sustained relationship* in which two people enter into a more intense teaching and learning experience, and then eventually separate. Some of these relationships will be friendships and others, professional or romantic. If you open yourselves up and try not to make marriage the outcome in these romantic relationships, you will go through experiences that will provide you both with lessons for your personal growth. Many of us experience this type of romantic relationship, but have difficulty with the physical separation that will and should happen. Know that physically the relationship will appear to have ended, but mentally and spiritually the relationships will provide long-lasting change in your life. That's why it's important to never abandon the person when you're leaving the relationship. Don't treat the ex like a second-class citizen. It's essential that we honor the eternal nature of relationships. If a person ends the physical aspects of a relationship properly, you then can go into your next relationship with a stronger capacity to love, from a healed, whole place. When a marriage ends, it could be that there are no longer any opportunities for mutual growth. People tend to view these marriages as failures; in reality, if both people learned what they were supposed to learn from each other, then it was a successful relationship!

The third level of teaching is for relationships that last all of our lives, because the other person provides us with unlimited opportunities for learning and growing. These relationships will teach us a lifetime of lessons. Just by the mere fact that these individuals are in our lives forces us to grow and become better individuals. These relationships don't happen frequently; instead, single women tend to spend too much time and effort trying to create this type of lifelong relationship with every new man they meet. By doing this, we set ourselves up for continual disappointment every time a relationship ends.

The Majority of Your Relationships WILL Come to an End – Prepare for It

Ladies, please do not lose your mind when a relationship ends. Most of your relationships will end, unless you get married, and sometimes even that relationship is terminated by divorce. I'm not trying to be pessimistic, but it's the truth.

Every relationship does not have to last forever; that may be setting your hopes too high right now. It's too much pressure, particularly if you're not with the right person. Living happily ever after may not be something you can work out; it simply might not be attainable. Sometimes you meet guys with whom you have a loving relationship for just a season. You may meet a man when you're on the rebound, and the short relationship is perfect and just what you need at that time. Those relationships can literally help bring you back to life.

If you are in an unfulfilling relationship that is wrong for you, don't be afraid to end it. A sure sign that it's probably falling apart is if you are desperately trying to keep the relationship together. The harder that you're trying, the more likely this is.

Men have a better ability to get out of relationships than women. Oftentimes a man will give you clues long before he actually breaks up with you. For instance, the man starts to spend less time with you and has less sex with you. He also picks fights so he has an excuse to leave. Since the guy knows he's about to go, he may have already started seeing someone else.

During the pre-breakup phase, pay attention and prepare yourself to move on. Start working out and keep busy because breakups are always a tough time in your life. You will mourn the end of the relationship and allow yourself to do so.

You must realize that falling in love means that you take the risk of being hurt. That is the risk you take, but it is worth the risk. Don't let fear of being hurt prevent you from getting involved in deep meaningful relationships. It will be important to feel the pain. By allowing ourselves to feel the pain, hurt and sometimes rejection, we grow stronger as well as identify ways to improve ourselves for the next relationship. Pain in life is inevitable so learn how to feel and heal from these painful experiences in life.

CHAPTER TWENTY FOUR

The Truth about "Open" Relationships

The rules of traditional relationships require that you be emotionally and sexually exclusive to one person forever. Therefore, many people in committed relationships are monogamous by default, not by choice. We learn through society that monogamy is what everyone is doing, and thus it is what's expected in relationships. We are socialized to believe that true happiness can be achieved only in monogamous relationships. Even though this goes against many people's natural inclinations, they accept and buy into it. However, many folks are realizing that it is unrealistic to expect one person to fulfill all of their needs—emotional, sexual, spiritual, psychological, intellectual, financial, romantic, etc.

Some people have spent the majority of their life dealing with the fact that they have struggled to be monogamous and keep their desires under lock and key. They have often found themselves in situations of betrayal, cheating or unfaithfulness. Well, the strongest argument for non-monogamy is that one person *cannot* fulfill all of our needs. In fact, for some people who have great physical, spiritual and emotional needs, it is unrealistic for one person to fulfill all of those needs and desires. This often sets us up for disappointment when a partner can't meet all of our expectations. In fact, open relationships can often prevent us from unhealthy co-dependent relationships, e.g. relationships that we stay in for fear of being without the person at all.

Cheating on one's spouse or mate has become a part of our culture, and even though it is not perceived as acceptable, it is still practiced by a large number of people. In contrast, in open relationships, all parties involved agree to be honest and open about their desires and needs instead of cheating, lying and being deceptive with their partner.

Open relationships are committed, but nonexclusive relationships, that involve some degree of intimacy with multiple partners. These relationship arrangements, also referred to as "responsible non-monogamy," can be applied to both married and unmarried couples.

An open relationship provides an alternative to being a traditional couple; under this arrangement, both partners can agree that each may engage in extramarital sexual relationships, without this being regarded as infidelity. Also, I want to point out that there are many different types of open relationships. In some open relationships, either the primary pairing or the outside relationships are not about sex; they may just include companionship, intimacy and compassion. That is why you'll often hear these relationships referred to as "intimate friendships." The key factor is that open relationships provide the opportunity to have intimate friendships with multiple people in an ethical and responsible way.

Open relationships provide an opportunity to get to know, love and experience different people in your life. To determine if open relationships are right for you, you will need to do lot of soul-searching and self-analysis to come to your own conclusion. You'll need to consider what you believe about monogamy and open relationships.

Redefining Marriage Relationships

There are alternatives for the millions of men and women who are failing at traditional marital relationships and feel guilty or ashamed about their ongoing relationship challenges. In the past, whenever there was infidelity or a desire for one partner to be intimate with someone else, the primary option considered was divorce or to end the relationship. One must think that there has to be more imaginative alternatives other than divorce.

Open marriages provide an alternative in which both partners agree that each may engage in extramarital sexual relationships, without this being regarded as infidelity. There are many different types of open marriages based upon the partners having varying levels of input about their spouse's activities. An open marriage is one in which each partner has room for personal growth and can develop outside friendships. These nonexclusive relationships involve some degree of intimacy, whether it be emotional, physical/sexual, or intellectual. I would recommend the book called *Open Marriage* by Nena O'Neill and George O'Neill for more information.

Many people will openly say that they don't agree with open marriages, while secretly desiring alternative relationships outside of their marriage. Given that over 3.2 million members have joined www.Ashleymadison.com, a website for extramarital affairs with married people only, I think many people are already pursuing open marriages but just have not openly acknowledged it.

Many who participate in open marriages have identified the following benefits:

- An opportunity to grow as separate individuals while maintaining a supportive love for each other, which, in turn, can cause the union to grow stronger and richer by adding outside experiences

- The excitement of living in the present and experiencing new opportunities and people who help us grow as individuals

- Being free to get different needs met with different people without having to end one relationship to start another

Open marriages provide an opportunity to get to know, love and experience different people in your life. To be clear, open relationships are not primarily about casual or sport sex. There are numerous ways to love someone; the act of sex is the easy part. Have you ever had a mind-blowing, intense conversation with a stranger, an innocently felt strong desire to see them again? This special type of connection is not about sex, it's about a natural attraction for this person. In fact, there are numerous ways to make love or create intimacy with another person without ever having sex with them. Some of my most intimate moments with my husband were just cuddling the entire night. Partners in open relationships are willing to engage in committed, serious relationships with more than one person, whether that be a friend, lover or online pal.

Don't misunderstand me; I believe that there are definite benefits from the security, warmth and stability of a nurturing family. However, we must find new ways to create and sustain intimate relationships that meet our intrinsic needs. For many people, it is very natural for them to desire sexual intimacy with more than one partner. This intrinsic desire is why so many monogamous relationships fail. There is a conflict between the person's natural non-monogamous nature and the monogamous tradition, and this conflict should cause us to explore new forms of intimate relationships.

Types of Open (Marriage) Relationships

Couples in open marriages may prefer different kinds of extramarital relationships. The two most popular open marriage relationships are polyamory and swinging. Couples who prefer extramarital relationships emphasizing love and emotional involvement with another person have a polyamorous style of open marriage; couples who seek extramarital relationships emphasizing sexual gratification and recreational friendships have a swinging style of open marriage. Polyamory focuses on love and the emotional relationship with other lovers, whereas swinging is often recreational sex, with an explicit intention to avoid an emotional connection.

Polyamory

Polyamory is motivated by a desire to expand love by developing emotionally involved relationships with extramarital partners. Polyamory is about stable intimate, emotionally committed relationships rather than casual sex. It is not a synonym for promiscuity. This is about having multi-partner relationships that are stable, consensual, responsible and nurturing.

A key factor in polyamorous relationships is the understanding of the primary relationship and secondary relationship. The primary relationship is the committed,
long-term marriage type relationship between two primary
partners. These primary partners are typically legally married and have decided to be committed to each other for
life. The primary partners generally live together and
share financial responsibilities, parenting and other key life
decisions, and they are considered each other's immediate
family. The secondary relationship may also be long-term,
but the partners generally don't live together and manage
their finances separately; they consider themselves as close,
intimate friends, but not immediate family.

Swinging

Swinging is defined as recreational sexual activity, also
called sport sex or wife swapping. Basically the couples
agree to have casual sex with each other. There is usually
no emotional involvement. Swinging is motivated by a
desire for physical gratification by engaging in sexual activities with extramarital partners. Swingers generally practice recreational sex activities without the development of
love, affection or personal intimacy. Some say swinging
replicates the dating pattern of the unmarried, but on a
couple basis.

Impact of Open Marriages

The impact of open marriages on relationships really
varies across couples. Some couples report high levels of
marital satisfaction and have long-lasting open marriages.
Other couples maintain open relationships for a season,
but later return to sexual monogamy. Oftentimes, these

couples continue to believe open marriage is a valid lifestyle, but just not for them. However, some couples experience serious problems and claim their open marriage lifestyle contributed to their divorce. It is not fully understood why some couples respond positively to open marriage while other couples respond negatively.

Is Open Marriage Adultery?

Adultery is not merely a sexual act. In fact, in the Bible, Israel committed adultery against God on numerous occasions, so that means there is probably more to adultery than it only being about sex.

Adultery has always been and currently is about breaking the marriage bond. This not only includes sexual infidelity, but emotional infidelity as well. So if a husband and wife do not "bind" themselves to sexual exclusivity with one another, then for them, extra-marital sex will not be adultery.

Many men in the Bible, such as David, Gideon, Abraham and Solomon, had sex with many women they were not married to, but none of them was accused of adultery. There were great men in the Bible who God approved of that had sex with many different women. God used these men mightily for His purposes and even developed special relationships with them.

Even in the New Testament, Jesus' teaching around adultery seems to focus on breaking the marriage bond. So, if you divorce (i.e., get rid of one's spouse and break the marriage covenant) and remarry without just cause, that constitutes adultery.

The basis for marriage is lifetime commitment to each other. Having sex with someone other than your spouse does not necessarily imply anything about that commitment. God asks that a man or woman honor their marriage commitment and maintain the covenant unless one partner is unfaithful to the vows that binded them together. If sex with another person does not threaten the marriage bond, then it is not an issue.

Therefore, if a married couple maintains mutual commitment with each other, they can still be open to pursue sexual or intimate friendships. Open marriages maintain the commitment to one another as practiced in traditional monogamy, but resolved the challenges some couples face around sexual exclusivity.

We all can admit that traditional monogamy is in crisis, and it is being mocked by the incredible high divorce rate. Of course, for those who desire traditional monogamy, traditional marriage will always be an acceptable alternative. However, there are options for those who wish to explore alternatives for their marriage relationships.

I know the truth shall set you free. If you research and study and let God be your guide, you can achieve sexual freedom without the baggage of misinformation and incorrect teachings. Finding Biblical truth is no small task, but it's definitely worth the effort. You will always be richly rewarded by finding God's truth in your life.

Are Open Relationships or an Open Marriage Right for You?

There are certain personality traits and situations that seem best suited for this type of lifestyle. Assess the points below to determine if an open marriage can work for you:

* **High self-esteem:** You have to be really secure and self-confident to be willing to share your partner with someone else. If you are already insecure in the relationship or are always seeking other people's acceptance, then an open marriage relationship probably won't work for you.

* **Natural talent for establishing intimate relationships:** Some people are gifted at athletics or singing, while some are gifted at establishing close intimate friendships with people. If you enjoy giving and receiving affection, and getting close to people, you have a talent for establishing intimate friendships. To contrast that, there are some who are challenged to sustain intimacy and meaningful relations with one person.

* **Desire diversity:** If you are interested in people's unique differences in terms of personality, intellect, or physical size/shape, then open marriage relationships may provide the opportunity for more diversity in your life.

* **Strong communication and interpersonal skills:** Open relationships require that you communicate honestly and candidly; it is necessary to have solid communication and people skills, due to the complex nature of these relationships.

207

🔹 **Mismatched desire for sex:** If one of the partners has a high sex drive or one is uninterested in sex, then an open marriage relationship may solve the mismatched desire for sex and provide a viable alternative.

🔹 **Focus on continual personal and spiritual growth:** If relationships are seen as opportunities for personal and spiritual growth, then having multiple intimate relationships will definitely accelerate your development in these areas.

You Decide What's Best for You

In life, change is inevitable. As we grow and evolve as human beings, so do our needs, desires and wants in life. By learning to embrace the changing nature of relationships, we have less to fear and lose because we never have to break up in the traditional sense. Open relationships grow and evolve in different directions over time. We can choose to live with a partner, and never marry, we can decide to get married, and we can decide to have kids or not to have kids. It may be suitable for you to decide if an open relationship is right for you. You can decide the best way to foster healthy and responsible relationships that work for you.

Open relationships provide an opportunity to get to know, love and experience different people in your life. To determine if open relationships are right for you, you will need to do lot of soul-searching and self-analysis to come to your own conclusion. You'll need to consider what you believe about monogamy and open relationships. To read more about open relationships and determine if they are right for you, visit my website at jjsmithonline.com to download more detailed information on the subject.

CHAPTER TWENTY FIVE

Conclusion

Dating Is a Competitive Sport – Learn to Enjoy It!

D ating is a sport and we know that men love sports. So for them, dating is generally fun and enjoyable. However, too many women don't want to have fun dating, they just want to find a husband. If your only focus in life is to find a husband, you will miss all the enjoyment and personal development opportunities that dating adds to your life.

So you will have to learn how to get in the dating game, compete, and have fun! Because dating is a sport, you will have to practice dating until you become in control of your dating life. Just like an athlete trains and practices to compete and win, you will have to practice to begin to win the dating game and achieve the results you desire.

If you are divorced or over thirty-five, dating for you has its own advantages. By now, you should be much clearer on what you need and want out of a relationship. On the home front, you likely have no one to answer to but yourself, and you can spend this time, maybe for the first time, thinking about what you want and need out of life. We've all heard that women reach their sexual prime in their thirties, so by this time, you should be more confident in your body and sexuality. Don't worry about not having a young perky body. You're likely to be more financially stable, so you can afford to pay for a trainer or for cosmetic surgery to tighten things up—if that makes you feel more confident with your body. If you are not as financially established, there are places that offer free or low cost gym memberships (e.g., the YMCA) and several books that you can buy to learn how to get in great shape. You have the freedom and flexibility to live your life the way you want, how you want, and where you want. This is the time to enjoy your newfound freedom and follow your heart wherever it leads you. It is never too late to reinvent yourself and have the life that you've always wanted.

After experiencing the joys and pains of dating and married life, I finally feel that I am happy and fulfilled. As a result of my journey over the years, I have a deeper relationship with God, a loving family, wonderful friends, a great career, good credit, a tone body and optimal health. I am finally winning the dating game and have plenty of male companionship to add fun and excitement to my life.

When I date, I have no pre-conceived ideas on what the outcome should be. Personally, I am not looking to get married again, but I'm not opposed to the idea either. If I meet someone who makes me feel that being married to them is better than the luxuries of my single life, then I would consider getting married again. The most important thing to me is to have quality, meaningful relationships with men with similar dreams, goals and interests in life.

As you begin to change your views and approach to dating, be enthusiastic about the process. Some of the strategies in this book will work well for you and others will not.

Life is a process of trying different things; if one thing doesn't work, then try something else until you achieve your goals. Be prepared to run into obstacles, and when you do, maintain your enthusiasm and energy level through this process and don't get discouraged. Be open to new experiences and expect to fail a few times as you began to take control of your dating life.

The secret is to keep moving forward, despite the failures and setbacks. Take it one day at a time, have fun along the way, and eventually you will have manifested the life and the love you desire!

Action Item
The 30 Day Action Challenge:

For the next 30 days, select a different action item from the book each day. The goal is to begin to change your daily habits to move yourself toward creating the life you want and attracting love into your life.

Acknowledgments

M om and Dad, thanks for giving me every opportunity to succeed in life. The two of you have given me wisdom, strength and encouragement, and you made me know God when I was little, whether I wanted to or not. Mom, you provide me with a model of a beautiful queen every day. Don't ever change!

Todd, my best friend who I love so dearly. No one outside of my family has loved me as much as you do. If you get one great love in a lifetime, for me, you are it!

To my brothers, Jay, Johnny and (cousin) Troy, thanks for loving and protecting me throughout my life. Jay, thanks especially for always encouraging me in everything I do; you have always supported and encouraged me, and never judged me... and I have had some crazy a#@!& ideas!

To my uncles—Eugene, Thomas, Edward and Spencer—all of you showed me what it is to provide for and take care of a family.

To my aunts—Elsie, Aggie, Sandy, Maggie, Connie, Theresa and Judy—all of you showed me how to love and care for a man. Both my aunts and uncles have shown me love since the day I was born.

To my cousins, who grew up with me like sisters—Karen, Tina, Vickie, Darlene, Tiffany, Lashanda, Rhonda, Cheryl and Cassandra. Some of my most memorable times in life have been with all of you. Thanks to all of my other cousins and two very special cousins, Kenny and Kathy, who have loved, supported and encouraged me all my life.

To my Godbrother and his family - J.R. and Lequisha (Qui), thanks for loving me and giving me feedback (whether it's good or bad) to help me grow and be a better person. Your beautiful family is a role model to me and so many others!

To my best girlfriend, Bridget. You have made life's journey over the years fun and enjoyable. Every part of my life has been influenced and made better by you.

To my entire Intact family—I'm fortunate to have had the opportunity to work with some of the smartest people who I have ever met in my lifetime—Todd, Jesse, Salena, Derek, Sherrie, and all the other Intact team members.

To my favorite men in my life who make every day at work fun and enjoyable at 1200K—Eric B. (thanks for watching my back!), Mike C. (mayor), Russ B. (comedian), and Brian G. (motivator). The four of you thoroughly entertain and care for me each and every day. You guys make coming to work too much fun. You are truly my extended family for life. A special thanks to Mike C. and Russ B. who provided me with candid feedback to ensure that this book was all I wanted it to be!

To my other friends at 1200K, thanks for providing a wonderful supportive work environment—Deborah H., Ken O., Patsy G., Mike G., Vera P., Carlos R., John M., Scott B., Jim

K., Ric M., Duane B., Clyde E., Nasser S., Connie O., Vidhya S., Greg D., Terry B., Samuel N., Jeanette D., LaTonya E., Bruce T., Jesse J., Jesse K., Marc F. and Cross C. and my friends that provide me with the most fun of my workdays, The Coalition.

Thanks to my thoughtful, talented editor, Robin Quinn, who went above and beyond and constantly exceeded my expectations. My appreciation also goes to my gifted book cover designer, George Foster. To Irene Archer, my Interior Designer, thanks for making each and every page of this book look so wonderful! Thanks for all your efforts. To Roy Cox, my incredible photographer who just didn't take photos of me, but made me feel like a supermodel. Thanks for making the photoshoot a memorable experience.

There are some people who have helped me in more ways than they even realized. Jamie Foxx, Marcus King, and Guy Black – I'm grateful for the opportunity you provided me! It has allowed so many other doors to be opened for me. Thank you!

To the women who I have never met that inspire me each and every day—Oprah Winfrey, Michelle Obama, and Hillary Clinton.

To all the men who I dated and loved over the years, as you have inspired me to write my very first book. You have given me more than enough material for this book and I thank you for that!

And, last but not least, thanks to my Lord and Savior, Jesus Christ, for giving me an abundant life!

About the Author

J.J. Smith is a dating expert, radio personality, passionate life coach, inspirational speaker and corporate executive in the D.C. metro area. J.J. is the host of an internet radio show called "Real Talk with JJ and The Fellas," which offers an intelligent, provocative and somewhat shocking look at love, dating, sex and relationships. Today through her seminars, small group workshops, and personal one-on-one relationship coaching sessions, J.J. is helping women of all ages upgrade the quality of their personal relationships with men.

J.J. Smith's dating and relationship expertise is in high demand, with recent appearances on the "Jamie Foxx Show," the "Michael Baisden Show," "Montel Williams: Montel Across America," the "Guy Black Show " and "Alluring Looks," an online beauty and style magazine. J.J. has been featured on the WNBC Weekend Today Show and recently been interviewed by Glamour Magazine and the Ladies Home Journal. J.J. has provided dating tips and relationship advice on several radio shows, including HOT 97 and KISS 98.7 in New York City. J.J.'s engaging personality, and no-holds barred dating books offer sometimes controversial guidance that has been grabbing readers and listeners, both men and women alike, and keeping them coming back for more.

This current work, *Why I Love Men: The Joys of Dating*, is J.J.'s first book. It includes the compelling and funny story of her love relationships with men over the past 15 years. In a sister-to-sister, woman-to-woman, friend-to-friend manner, the author shares the heartfelt story of her joys, pains and lessons learned from dating. *Why I Love Men* is ultimately a tribute to men and how they have shaped her life and helped her to grow and develop as a woman.

J.J. holds a B.A. in Mathematics from Hampton University in Virginia. She continued her education by completing The Wharton Business School Executive Management certificate program. She currently serves as Vice President and Partner in an IT Consulting firm, Intact Technology, Inc. J.J. was also the youngest African-American to receive a Vice President position at a Fortune 500 company. She is the recipient of several performance awards and has published numerous white papers and eBooks. J.J. is a gifted speaker and a certified seminar leader. Her hobbies include reading, writing and deejaying.

Share Your Stories and Lessons Learned!

If you'd like to share your dating experiences or lessons learned, please feel free to contact the author, J.J. Smith, and she would be glad to hear from you!

If you have questions or comments about the book, the author can be reached at:

J.J. Smith, www.jjsmithonline.com
12138 Central Ave, Ste. 391
Mitchellville, MD 20721
Email: info@jjsmithonline.com

Special Bonus eBooks

If you'd like more information on some of the topics discussed in this book, please see my website at www.jjsmithonline.com.

The following bonus eBooks can be found on my website:

- 40 is the New 30: How to Look 10 Years Younger!
- 101 Best Places to Meet Men
- 200+ Online Dating Sites: Find a Site Targeted Specifically for You!
- Understanding Open (Marriage) Relationships
- Why I Love My Dad: Things a Father Must Teach His Daughter
- Why I Love Men: Companion Workbook

LaVergne, TN USA
30 September 2009
159537LV00001B/1/P